Roots *&*
Branches

St. Willibrord Community Credit Union

The first 50 years

Mark Kearney & Otte Rosenkrantz

Canadian Cataloguing in Publication Data

Rosenkrantz, Otte, 1952-
Roots and Branches: St. Willibrord Community Credit Union, The First Fifty Years

Includes bibliographical references and index.
ISBN 0-9687045-0-6 (bound) ISBN 0-9687045-1-4 (pbk.)

1. St. Willibrord Community Credit Union – History. I. Kearney, Mark, 1955- .
II. St. Willibrord Community Credit Union. III. Title.

HG2039.C2R67 2000 334'.22'097132 C00-931005-3

Cover Design: Connections Integrated Communications Inc.
Colour Staff and Branch photos: Richard Bain Photography
Editorial Consulting: Ergo Productions
Index: Robert J. Graham

Typeset, printed, and bound in Canada by
The Aylmer Express Limited
Aylmer, Ontario

Acknowledgements

We wish to acknowledge and thank the large number of people who contributed time, energy, talent, personal memories, and enthusiasm to *Roots and Branches*.

Anne Callon
Janet Taylor
Erin McMordie
Karen Hardy
Lisa Kennedy
Patricia Hoeksema
Tina Van Loon
Karen Willemse and Tracy Maschke: Archival Help
Richard Bain
Win Schell and Linda Gregson
Robert J. Graham
Frans Schryer
John and Lena Strybosch
Andreas Strubin
Wilma Bastiaansen
Ted Smeenk
Gerald and Annie Sanders
Janet Anderson and Kees Govers
Frederica Vanbrock
Rose Bakker
The late Nick Van Osch
Individual Branch Managers and Staff of St. Willibrord, as well as the many others who were interviewed, and provided us with photos and illustrations.

Thank you all!
Mark Kearney and Otte Rosenkrantz

"The persistent one wins."

— Dutch proverb

Table of Contents

Introduction

A New Life in Southwestern Ontario

About fifteen billion years ago, give or take an epoch or two, our local universe started expanding from a very small space at light speed, and it's still growing. Plasma cooled, atomic particles formed, protons, neutrons and electrons found each other and started their quantum mechanical dance. They gathered into atoms and molecules, cooled further and started coalescing and clumping into clusters and galaxies.

About five billion years ago, our local solar system was well on its way to adopting its current structure, and our earth and its moon started their orbital and tidal dance. Fast forward another billion years or two when winds and tides and all kinds of other factors shaped the setting and stirred the primordial soup in which, perhaps "salted" with extraterrestrial seeds and perhaps with a divine spark or guidance, amino acids first started combining in ever-increasing complexity and produced ... LIFE.

Primitive life forms kept combining and evolving and adapting to the current environment, or died trying. Sometimes, wittingly or unwittingly, these life forms even changed their own environment, triggering another round of evolution, adaptation and ever-increasing complexity.

Fast forward almost to today, cosmically speaking. The ancestors of the first Homo sapiens start to stand tall on two legs and hold tools in their hands with opposable thumbs. Their minds form the first ideas and concepts and then create languages to communicate them. They paint pictures on cave walls and pass stories from generation to generation. Cooperative practices emerge in their behaviour and make it possible to hunt and gather more efficiently, to live in communities and generate their own future security.

Wait. Hold on. What does all this "life and evolution" business have to do with the story of a credit union? Change the nouns in the preceding four paragraphs but keep the verbs and adjectives, rearrange the order a bit, and you have a description of the birth, growth, and ongoing development and evolution of a new kind of life in Southwestern Ontario. That organism, or organization if you prefer, is called St. Willibrord Community Credit Union. The purpose of *Roots and Branches* is to describe this new form of life, and it does so by telling the story of its first 50 years.

Most descriptions of companies, to date, have been phrased in mechanical terms, but successful organizations do not, or should not, view themselves that way any more. A company, or to be more specific in this case, a cooperative credit union and St. Willibrord in particular, is more like a complex life form than like any machine. Each person has a special place within the whole, performing a unique function, often as part of a team, contributing to the long-term survival of the group as well as thriving individually.

In fact, that is what happened 50 years ago in Southwestern Ontario. Immigrants came to a new land as prepared as they could, or were allowed to be, to start a new life; but something was missing. A secure and supportive gathering place to meet personal, financial needs. One person stopped to consider the possibilities. Word went out. He held a meeting. People attended and shared their views. At the end of the evening, 20 of them signed a special piece of paper. The seed had been planted and a short while later, less than three months, the credit union was "born".

For the organization to grow, attract, and process the resources necessary to fulfill its purpose, it needed to be nourished as well as cultivated. More and more people joined. The organism grew, sometimes in fits and starts, and slowly, as befitted the pace of the times. Then, the climate changed abruptly and, to survive, the youthful credit union found it necessary to undertake an evolutionary leap or two, adapting to the new circumstances, adjusting its own internal structure, experimenting with new ways of doing things.

All along the way, each community cluster, group, or branch within the credit union developed its own unique culture and atmosphere, tuned to the needs and desires of its constituents, but still part of the overall organization and within its regional boundaries.

How did the organism do all this? First, it developed the capacity for using more complex tools, leading to an increased comfort with adopting the latest technology. When what was available on the shelf did not quite fit the bill, it broke new ground and started developing some applications of its own. Second, it developed a language, a structure, and a culture of building consensus, making decisions for the mutual benefit of both individuals and the collective, along with a commitment to keep communicating openly and exploring options until one could be found, acceptable to all, and implemented.

As I write this, the credit union is almost fifty years young. The environment is changing again, fast, ultra fast. It is changing so much that we are entering not just a new age or a new land but a whole new world. How will this life form fare in the new world? Is it prepared? What will happen? What will it look like? How long will it last?

George Santayana, the philosopher and poet, is recorded as saying, "Those who are ignorant of the past are doomed to repeat it." While we must know about and understand our past, we cannot afford to repeat it. Don't get me wrong. Our past wasn't bad. It was actually quite good, but some old practices will just not work in the present time.

St. Willibrord is not looking ahead on the same time scale as noted at the beginning of this introduction, but let's, instead, consider the next five, ten, or fifty years. I cannot tell you exactly what will happen. No one can. I can, however, reassure you that St. Willibrord is ready, able, and willing to tackle the future. We're looking forward to it. It's going to be fun!

Where does that combination of optimism, confidence and enthusiasm originate? It is built into the life of the organization and to understand that, you need the whole story. *Roots and Branches* is about people, their personal stories of struggle and achievement, and how these have all contributed to that unique, complex, adaptive life form called St. Willibrord Community Credit Union.

Harry Joosten
Vice President – Owner Relations & Corporate Secretary
St. Willibrord Community Credit Union
March 2000

Prologue

When Gerald Sanders contemplates how successful St. Willibrord Community Credit Union has been over the past half century, he has just one piece of advice to offer the credit union for the future, "Don't ever become a bank." He is, of course, referring to the personal touch all St. Willibrord members experience when they visit their credit union. "Ever since I first started doing business with St. Willibrord, I have felt welcomed there. They know me and treat me as an individual."

Sanders first encountered St. Willibrord in 1969 when he needed to borrow money to buy a tractor. There were two choices: the branch of the bank where he had been doing business in the past, or the local branch of St. Willibrord where he also had an account. "I decided to go see John Strybosch in Arkona. I told him that I didn't have a lot of money - Annie and I had just been married for a year and we were just starting out - and I'll never forget what he said, 'Today we help you, Mr. Sanders, and tomorrow you can help us.' And then he approved the loan."

Gerald Sanders with children Mike and Lori-Anne, 1972

When it came time to purchase his farm three years later, Sanders went to a bank where he believed he was already qualified for a farm loan. Much to his surprise, the local branch manager refused his request for the loan, and referred the matter to the main office in Toronto, where it was refused again. "You can imagine my surprise," he notes. "Here I thought I was already approved for a loan with a good rate, and I was refused."

Once again, he turned to St. Willibrord and received his money. "After that, I went back to the bank, asked them what I owed them, paid them off, and closed my account there. I never went back." Over the years, Sanders, who now runs a highly successful farming operation, would make several subsequent loans, always from St. Willibrord. "I must have bought 30 tractors since then," he says with a laugh.

This kind of experience with St. Willibrord is one echoed by many other members of the credit union since its inception in 1951. Willing to take into consideration the personalities and the individual potential of loan applicants, St. Willibrord, time and again, approved loans to individuals who took advantage of this show of faith and trust to turn their enterprises into success stories. Over the years, and compared to other financial institutions, St. Willibrord has historically experienced very few defaulted loans. On occasion, loans have been renegotiated or extended to allow the borrower extra time, but the people who have brought their business to this particular financial institution have invariably found a willing, sympathetic ear, and an attitude of cooperation.

According to Sanders, his wife Annie, and other members, St. Willibrord developed a unique attitude toward customer service because its philosophy was rooted in the belief that a credit union exists to help people. Annie's father was John Hendrikx, one of the original Dutch Catholic immigrants involved in the development of the credit union. "It was important to him to help the newcomers," she recalls, "because he knew how hard it had been for many of them to get money to make a new life in Canada." Annie also notes that it was important in the early days that the people who operated the credit union were themselves immigrants who spoke Dutch. "They were in a unique position to help the people who came to Canada later. There was a sense of community and family and trust you just didn't find anywhere else."

"You also knew the people you were going to deal with," adds Gerald. "John Willemse was in Arkona for something like fourteen years, and I was always very comfortable doing business with him. You could walk in, sit down and talk about anything before having to get down to business. I like that." Like so many others, Sanders comments that the people who work behind the counter go to considerable trouble to know you, and to be helpful.

Sanders eventually found his involvement with the credit union move beyond being a member. "When John Hendrikx retired after 25 years, he asked me to consider running for his place on the branch council in Arkona. It was quite an honour." After serving on that committee, he was invited by Strybosch to become a member of the credit committee in Arkona, and served for seven years. In that capacity, he learned firsthand what it was that made St. Willibrord so popular with its members.

Gerald and Annie Sanders, February 2000

"It is hard to believe how poor many of the Dutch immigrants were back then, in the late 40s, and early 50s," recalls Annie. "I can remember some kids having bailing twine for belts and tin cans to drink from. The first year we lived in Parkhill, the snow blew in through the kitchen windows. We lived in the front part of the house. I remember the stove sitting in the middle of the living room. With 13 children, things were pretty tough for my parents for quite a while, but they never looked back, and they never regretted their decision to come." With St.Willibrord acting as both financial institution and *de facto* social organization, the young Dutch immigrants found a welcome in Southwestern Ontario that would make them feel at home. Like many other St. Willibrord members, Annie and Gerald met at a dance put on by the Dutch immigrants, most of whom were members of the credit union.

Over the years, the Sanders had occasion to go to the credit union for loans to purchase everything from farmland and equipment to livestock and crop seed. Now, almost 30 years after borrowing money for their first tractor, Annie and Gerald can look with pride at the land and farms they own, and all they have accomplished. As well, their children, three daughters and a son, are all members of the credit union.

"You can never tell how things are going to work out," says

Gerald. "But I am pretty sure things would not have worked out as well as they have were it not for St. Willibrord." Then he adds with a laugh, "What other financial institution is there where the branch manager will come right to your farm, bring the paperwork for a loan, have coffee, and know what he is talking about when he talks farming?" As Gerald Sanders notes, as long as St. Willibrord maintains that friendly, knowledgeable, personal touch that the original members insisted be part of the St. Willibrord philosophy back in 1951, it will continue to do well and attract new members.

To a New Land

CHAPTER 1

The story of St. Willibrord Community Credit Union begins more than 50 years ago, a long way from Southwestern Ontario, Canada.

After the Second World War (1939-45), people in the Netherlands were faced with enormous challenges. The postwar era offered few opportunities to a new generation. Many industries and much of the infrastructure had been destroyed, housing was in short supply, jobs were scarce, and many feared that the farmland which had supported their families for generations would not sustain a growing population.

At the same time, the War had left countries such as Canada, Australia, and New Zealand with a shortage of labour and expanding economies. Federal governments in Canada, under Prime Minister W.L. Mackenzie King and then Louis St. Laurent, developed policies designed to encourage immigration. On January 30, 1947, Canada amended its immigration regulations to provide for the admission of sponsored agriculturalists.

With promises of cheap land, good wages, and a supportive government, notices went out to many European countries, including the Netherlands, that Canada would welcome any people who were willing to work.

Dutch people remembered, as they do to this day, that Canadian forces had helped liberate their country. They also knew that Queen Juliana (then a Princess) had stayed in Canada for some of the war years. As well, many young women from the Netherlands came to Canada after the War to marry Canadian soldiers they had met in wartime. In 1946, the Canadian government had paid the passage for about 2,000 Dutch war brides and 400 children.

For a wide variety of reasons, 509,000 Dutch immigrants arrived in Canada between 1946 and 1978. About 20,000 came each year from 1951 to 1963. Most settled in Ontario although a large number travelled all the way to British Columbia.

Through books such as *Brabanders in Canada* by John H. Dortmans, people today may get intimate glimpses of the changes experienced by individuals who left the Netherlands and chose Canada. Few things are as difficult as trying to make a new life in a foreign land. When language and culture suddenly become barriers to finding work, making friends, and setting up a new home, the prospect of becoming established can seem overwhelming. The Dutch were used to living in close-knit communities which were connected to a rich cultural heritage. In Canada, they had to start almost everything all over again.

Imagine what it was like to leave close ties to a fairly homogeneous society and suddenly meet the much more culturally diverse population of Southwestern Ontario. Immigrants had left those they trusted in personal, business, and financial affairs but met others who spoke a new language, had different associations, customs, and community leaders. There was one interesting exception. Many Flemish Catholic (Belgian) immigrants had settled in this area after the First World War, and they welcomed to their communities new immigrants from the Netherlands. Since the Flemish and Dutch languages were quite similar, communication was easy.

The co-op system, which was familiar and well-developed in the Netherlands, was not nearly as established here. In the beginning, without traditional co-op resources, new immigrants sought out people they could trust, friends of friends, usually Dutch or Flemish speakers who might help them in business and personal dealings.

Dutch immigrants were certainly not rich when they arrived, but most were by no means penniless. Despite efforts by the cash-poor Dutch government to limit amounts of currency taken out of the country, immigrants used their creativity to devise various methods of taking their hard-earned money with them. Many had sold farms, homes, and businesses before they left and those funds would be needed to start new lives in a new country.

Dortmans' book describes ingenious methods that some used to smuggle money out of the country. Paper currency was concealed in hollow legs of furniture, in packages of foodstuffs such as soup mixes or cornstarch, and hidden in dolls, Teddy Bears, shoulder pads, corsets, and brassières.

Many people had also prepared a "kist" or large wooden crate

Ready for planting on a farm near London in the 1950s

filled with belongings in preparation for leaving. Some brought smaller pieces of treasured furniture, linen, dishes, milk cans, rope, wooden shoes, and even rocks for the sauerkraut pot. But as many settlers discovered, new riches and security did not follow automatically upon arrival in Canada, despite their efforts to prepare for the experience. Letters back home from some immigrants, as noted by Dortmans, indicate that they felt poorly informed about the real Canada. Although land was indeed cheap, it was often heavy clay, hard to work or cultivate, and Ontario winters were more severe than expected. Moreover, a sheer willingness to work did not always guarantee a job, and the task of learning English from scratch was certainly not easy.

The Dutch who arrived in the late 1940s and early 1950s faced other surprises as well. Many who came here, usually because they were sponsored by someone, had to take jobs initially that were tough, not particularly prestigious, and for which they were often overqualified. Back-breaking farm labour, cleaning houses or business buildings, factory work, and odd jobs to make a few dollars here and there were just some examples of the work they took. But if menial jobs provided the only way to earn enough money to save for a farm, a business, a house, or a car, then most immigrants thought, "So be it."

John Féron, who later became Board president of St. Willibrord (1970-80), came to Canada as a young, single man in the 1950s, and saw firsthand what some families who immigrated had to endure. He

John Féron, Board President 1970-1980

FÉRON FAMILY MEMORIES

Like many other immigrant couples of the time, the Férons kept a close eye on expenses especially in the early days of their marriage: "There was no need for a car. I would walk to the bus, which I did for two and a half years. But our first priority was saving for a house. When we built our first house, it was only about 1,100 square feet. But I felt like it was a castle. I wrote home to my parents that I had built a house and that we were going to move in. The next year they had to come and see it. My father said, 'Now I see why you live in Canada.'

"At that time I was in charge of shipping and receiving at a London firm, so a good number of crates would come in and I would direct my driver to drop some of these empty crates off at my house. So the next weekend I was making little benches and tables for the kids to play with. But I never thought of buying these things which would cost money that you couldn't afford to spend.

"If you ask me if I had to do it over again, I would do it again. The other thing is, do you like what you have done? Yes, even with the tough times, we liked it."

offers some recollections of those early days in Canada. "Agriculture was very poor in the Netherlands, particularly in Brabant, where a good portion of the people were coming from. They also had large families. It ended up that there was a decision they were going to make. They were going to farm in Canada because Canada had lots of land and Canada had good potential. They were going to be farmers. That has worked for a good number of them, and we have all kinds of examples of a good solid development of families and farming. We also may not forget there was a price to pay for that. You come here with a big family and all were having to work for the farm. That meant that a good number of them were working in factories on the weekends to make extra money."

Féron notes how hard it was at the start for many immigrants: "Some of them were very disappointed, from the stories I have heard from people who had a big family having to live in a chicken coop, working in the fields of sugar beets. Being sent to farm and handled as slave labour, that type of thing. I personally have not experienced that for the simple reason that I was single when I came. So long as I had a sandwich and a bed, that's all I needed for the first few years.

"You stayed quite frequently at a small factory and tried to work up to owning a small farm. There were a good number of sacrifices made. But this immigration, I think, was a success. If you look around Southwestern Ontario, there is certainly the influence of the Dutch community."

Some Dutch women who had been used to running households in the Netherlands discovered that even their everyday task of grocery shopping was different in Canada. Local markets back home had been social gathering spots where prices were often established by good-humoured bargaining, haggling, and negotiating. A trip to a grocery store in Southwestern Ontario revealed a specific price tag on each item. The same, of course, applied to large department stores such as Eaton's or Simpson's which dominated the new furniture, clothing, and appliance market in those days. To some degree, no doubt, the fixed prices were an advantage for those whose English was not very strong. However, shopping here was a new process. And since it sometimes took older immigrants longer to learn English, their children who had been immersed in a new, English-speaking school system, often found themselves taking on important translation duties during shopping trips.

Harvesting the hay crop with the whole family

Immigrant women also encountered differences with regard to their traditional family roles which had been fairly well-defined in the Netherlands. In order to help their families build a nest egg to fulfill future dreams, women frequently secured employment that took them out of the home. With most working-age family members dedicated to a variety of jobs, sometimes in different towns or on different farms, women experienced the added stress of holding their families together. Different work schedules even made traditional, whole-family gatherings at dinner or supper less frequent and sometimes impossible.

There were also anxious times whenever a family member became ill or unemployed. Protection against sickness and unemployment had been taken for granted back in the Netherlands, but Canada's social safety net, which is now renowned everywhere, was not nearly as sophisticated or as widespread then. Immigrants often simply had to rely on themselves, their friends, and their parish priests.

The Roman Catholic Church was a welcome focal point for newly-arrived Dutch immigrants and in an effort to better serve the needs of thousands of newcomers from the Netherlands, Ontario Catholic bishops encouraged the immigration of a number of Dutch priests to help new immigrants with both social and spiritual matters. In January, 1950, a small seminary of the Priests of the Sacred Heart was established in Delaware, a community near London. One of the new priests' roles was to make Sunday visits to various communities in the area such as Delhi, Langton, Tillsonburg, and Aylmer. Meeting people in their community churches, the priests could take part in the Mass, hear confessions in Dutch, and offer general assistance or support.

For the Dutch and veteran Flemish immigrants, an annual "Dutch Picnic", sponsored by the priests in Delaware, was a welcome opportunity to meet a large number of those from their homeland in a beautiful setting. Hundreds attended these gatherings for Mass, Confession, and a rare chance to socialize with so many others experiencing the discovery of a new country and culture. While there appears to be no historical record, it is fair to speculate that many old friendships were renewed, much news from back home shared, and perhaps even a few courtships began around the legendary picnic baskets stuffed with delicious treats.

It is not surprising that the important role which Dutch priests played here in Southwestern Ontario would have spiritual, social, and economic effects on the local Dutch community. In fact, a charismatic and creative priest, Father Jan van Wezel, would be the driving force behind a move to establish a credit union in the Roman Catholic Diocese of London.

Another effort by the Church to help newcomers achieve success in Canada took the form of a booklet entitled *The Catholic Immigrant*, published in 1952. There are no records of how many people read this guide, but the range of advice is certainly interesting and down-to-earth, with a clear, practical focus. Dutch immigrants were urged to be flexible, willing to work, frugal in their ways, and responsible for fellow immigrants. They were also encouraged to keep their

WARNINGS, ADMONITIONS AND ADVICE FROM *THE CATHOLIC IMMIGRANT* (1952)

* Assimilation is necessary and more easily achieved by the younger generation. Learning the new language is therefore of the utmost importance; the courage to use it is paramount.
* For many immigrants, the dollar is the biggest danger. Some send their children to work in the city, a dangerous work milieu, only because they pay higher wages there. This can lead to abandonment of family life with the result that they will squander their money and no longer support their parents. It is better to earn less money and wait a bit longer for independence.
* Someone who wants to work will not meet anyone or anything as his obstacle. The work tempo in Canada is much faster than in the Netherlands. The immigrant must make the change immediately. One must never tell the employer that things in the Netherlands are better. Even if you ran your own business for years, don't forget who the employer is this time. Don't criticize and tell Canadians that in the Netherlands houses are better and streets cleaner.
* Go to Church every Sunday, whenever possible.
* Read the Bible with your children. Only adopt the good habits of the Canadians. Some regions have a terrible alcohol problem; guard yourself against this misery-causing practice.
* Some old immigrants are lax in their religious practices and give a poor example to newcomers.
* As a general rule, it is strongly recommended that you not emigrate as a single person. For the single person, the difficulties and dangers are too great. He will miss the moral support, the advice and the encouragement he needs. Due to lack of sufficient enjoyment of free time, as he knows it in the Netherlands, there is a danger that he will seek diversion in a fashion not fit for a Catholic. This will also make saving money impossible.
* Canada is the land of many opportunities for someone who is not afraid of difficulties, someone who can take advice, someone who lives frugally and in the beginning is satisfied with little comfort, someone who conducts himself in such a manner that the Canadians appreciate him.
* Be responsible for other immigrants. When one Dutchman bungles, the prestige of all Dutchmen suffers. Help one another. Many will be jealous of the other's success, incomprehensible but very true. Don't boast, and be sure to ask advice from people you can trust.
* Of absolute most importance for the emigrant is to keep up his Christian faith. The Dutch emigrant will most likely succeed in the financial sense, but in the religious-moral sense he does not have the same protection as he does in the Netherlands.

Christian faith, and be wary of the temptations of the dollar. No doubt, many of those leaving the Netherlands to come to Canada received heartfelt and sincere advice from friends and family before embarking on their journey.

As already noted, there were several general conditions which made it necessary and attractive for Dutch people to emigrate after the Second World War. They certainly came to this part of Canada with optimism, prepared as well as they could be, yet harbouring more than a few uncertainties and anxieties. A particular and personal side of the immigrant experience is given by John Strybosch who came to Ontario in July, 1951, and would later serve as General Manager of St. Willibrord from 1969 to 1988. As the oldest of eight children, Strybosch was 23 when his mother died and, when his father passed away a year later, he found himself solely responsible for his seven siblings: four sisters and three brothers. "As you can imagine, this was a very difficult time."

Strybosch also recalls, "The farm we lived on was near a small town that had been quite ravaged by the War. There was a lot of turmoil and uprooting as people tried to get used to the postwar world, and some had lost everything. As well, there were far too many people in the Netherlands and farm families often had 10 or 12 children. The early hope was that these children would also become farmers, but there simply was not enough land."

Not surprisingly then, interest was great when recruiters came from abroad to encourage emigration. Strybosch remembers the reception for one speaker from a company helping organize and promote emigration at a meeting in a local community hall. "The hall could hold 600 people at the most, but more than 1,000 came to listen."

What could the young head of a large household do? "There was a lot of talk in the town about emigrating, but I was scared. It was a step into the unknown. I knew what we were up against in the Netherlands and was not really convinced that things would be better anywhere else. My father had built up a good name in the community, and I just didn't want to leave that behind, as well as all our friends and other relatives. But my younger brothers and sisters were more optimistic and they really wanted to go. I was still unsure, but did feel it would be better to go as a family than to break up and go individually."

As it turned out, Strybosch's sister Josephine did decide to apply for immigration with her fiancé before the rest of the family had made a final decision to move. After her application was approved, she married and moved to Osgoode, near Ottawa, in 1950. But the first letters back from Josephine were not encouraging because they told stories of real hardship and unfriendly neighbours. They had landed in the middle of a severe Ottawa Valley winter without proper clothing and access to a car. This compounded the isolation felt because of the language barrier.

Through contact with an aunt in Watford, near London, Josephine and her husband Harry were able to move, and he got a job in a nearby feedmill. John Strybosch clearly remembers, "After the move to Watford, we began getting much more optimistic letters. That decided it for me. We packed up and moved and eventually found our way to Strathroy."

Strybosch still recalls the "high hopes and beautiful dreams", as well as doubts and questions going through his and other immigrants' minds: Will we be able to handle the work? Will I be missed? Will I see my loved ones again? Will we really be welcome or just considered aliens who take other people's jobs? Will I ever be able to start my own business? Will I be able to continue my studies in Canada? There were many questions, but all were related to the big question: What will the future hold for me?

One key ingredient to a successful future would be a financial institution or organization which understood immigrant concerns, their needs for a safe haven for carefully-saved money, their past experiences, and present dreams.

Many Dutch people weren't used to dealing with banks in the Netherlands, but had relied on a cooperative organization known as the Boerenleenbank or Farmers' Lending Bank. The cooperative system was a mainstay of Dutch rural society, and was familiar to farmers who immigrated here. They had been used to co-op banking, co-op feed mills, and a range of other services related to their livelihood.

It is understandable, then, that the concept of a credit union to serve Dutch Catholic immigrants in London and Southwestern Ontario would eventually be voiced and promoted here. The early 1950s would see the first stages of development for what is now well-known as the St. Willibrord Community Credit Union. Many of the modern pioneers eventually joined in this endeavour. Their energy, creativity, foresight, and courage are certainly still admired and respected by those who lead and belong to the credit union today.

ST. WILLIBRORD

Many present owners probably know that their credit union is named after the Patron Saint of the Netherlands. But who was St. Willibrord?

He was born in Northumbria, England, in about 658, and legend has it that his mother dreamed she swallowed a new moon the night she conceived him and was told by a priest that this meant her son would, "Walk in the splendour of heaven's light and reflect it in the full moon of his holiness."

At the age of six, as was common with young boys in those days, he was placed in the monastery at Ripon (northern England), under the care of St. Wilfred, after which he entered the Benedictine Order.

When he was twenty, he was sent to Ireland and spent twelve years in the Abbey of Rathmelsigni to study under St. Egbert of Iona. He studied for ten years, was ordained, and stayed at the Abbey for another two years.

Contemporaries described him as a faithful, hard-working monk who was physically strong, had dark hair, and clear, penetrating eyes.

In 690, Willibrord and eleven companions received permission from St. Egbert to travel as missionaries to pagan northern Germany. The next year, he and the other English monks undertook this dangerous mission. The Germans were fiercely loyal to their god Wotan, but their chief warlord, Pepin of Herstal, a nominal Christian, permitted the missionaries to preach. He encouraged them to go to Lower Friesland (the Netherlands), which Pepin had recently conquered and taken from the pagan Danish King Radbod. Although the Frisians were a ferocious tribe, Willibrord had considerable success in his mission, and finally Pepin recommended Pope Sergius I appoint him as Bishop. Sergius approved, consecrated him Bishop of Utrecht, and renamed him Clement. In some areas of the Netherlands he is still referred to as St. Clement.

Willibrord then extended his labours into Upper Friesland and Denmark. This region was still under the power of Radbod, a bitter enemy of Pepin. He met with only limited success because of strong resistance from Radbod. After destroying an idol on the island of Heligoland, he narrowly escaped the Danes with his life, and finally returned to Utrecht where he founded a monastery and built a cathedral. In 698, he established an abbey at the Villa Echternach (in what is now Luxembourg) on the River Sure before returning to his missionary work. In 715, Radbod recaptured Lower Friesland. He mercilessly slaughtered Christians and destroyed churches. Finally, Willibrord and his companions were forced to retreat to Germany where they continued their work among the Franks. In 719, Radbod died, and his successor permitted the return of the missionaries. At this time, Willibrord was joined by the young St. Boniface who would later convert the whole region.

Willibrord served as Bishop of Utrecht until he was almost eighty when he retired to the monastery at Echternacht. Although he had only nominal success in converting the Frisians, he was admired and respected by them for contributing to their well-being. He died peacefully at Echternacht in 739, at the age of eighty-one, and was buried in the oratory of the Abbey. After his death, he was almost immediately honoured as a saint.

St. Willibrord's feast is celebrated in the Netherlands on November 7, and, by order of Pope Leo XIII, on November 29 in England. Since his burial, Echternacht has been a place of pilgrimage, and miracles are said to have happened there. Each year since 1553, a group of pilgrims parades through the streets of Echternacht and across a bridge on the River Sure to the shrine of St. Willibrord. They dance four or five abreast, linked arm in arm, taking three steps forward and two back in time to traditional music, singing the refrain, "Heliger Willibrord, bitte für uns." (Holy Willibrord, pray for us.)

AT THE TIME

1945
- U.S. drops atomic bombs on Hiroshima and Nagasaki. August 6 and 9. Japan surrenders
- World War Two ends on August 14
- Charles De Gaulle elected President of French provisional government
- American General George S. Patton dies in automobile accident

1946
- United Nations General Assembly holds its first session in London, England
- Electronic "brain" built at Pennsylvania University
- Xerography process invented by Chester Carlson
- Joe Louis successfully defends World Heavyweight boxing title for the 23rd time

1947
- Belgium, the Netherlands, and Luxembourg ratify the Benelux customs union
- WW2 Peace Treaty signed in Paris
- Princess Elizabeth, heir to the British throne, marries Philip Mountbatten, Duke of Edinburgh
- U.S. airplane flies at supersonic speeds
- First reports of "flying saucers" in the United States

1948
- Jewish State of Israel comes into existence with Ben-Gurion as leader
- Queen Wilhelmina of the Netherlands abdicates and is succeeded by her daughter Juliana
- World Council of Churches organized in Amsterdam
- Legendary baseball player Babe Ruth dies

1949
- Apartheid policy established in South Africa
- The Netherlands transfers sovereignty to Indonesia
- George Orwell writes *Nineteen Eighty-four*
- Arthur Miller wins Pulitzer Prize for *Death of a Salesman*

1950
- World population reaches 2.3 billion
- There are 1.5 million television sets in the United States
- Senator Joe McCarthy advises President Truman that The State Department is riddled with Communists
- Antihistamines become popular remedy for colds and allergies
- Edgar Rice Burroughs, creator of Tarzan, dies
- Einstein explains his Theory of Relativity

Planting the Seed

CHAPTER 2

The foundation of what has become St. Willibrord Community Credit Union was envisioned by one man, Father Jan van Wezel. As Associate Director of Immigration for the Roman Catholic Diocese of London, his main task was to help immigrants with the transition from Dutch to Canadian society. Van Wezel would visit new arrivals in the countryside around London, counselling and helping them get settled. In the Netherlands, priests had wielded a lot of control and influence, and certainly they were people who could be trusted to take care of money. Dutch Catholics who were unfamiliar with Canadian banks, mistrustful of them, or simply unfamiliar enough with English to conduct business in that language, wanted someone trustworthy to handle their money. A priest seemed the logical choice.

Ted Smeenk, the credit union's first manager, (then called secretary/treasurer) recalls those early days. "Many dollars were smuggled in. What better way than to ask Father van Wezel to keep money for them in trust? Father van Wezel put the money safely in a bank and listed names of the owners on a scrap of paper. Through this process, he realized the potential of a credit union."

Exactly when van Wezel originated the plan for a credit union is not clear. But John Roks, who served on the credit committee during the 60s and 70s, remembers, "The first I heard about a credit union was quite possibly the first that anybody knew about it. I was in a car on November 4, 1950. I remember the date. Van Wezel talked for some reason about a credit union."

Van Wezel was the key figure in starting what was to become St. Willibrord Community Credit Union. He was such a charismatic figure that what he suggested carried a lot of clout with the newcomers. Credit unions had existed in Ontario for several decades, but had undergone some difficult times in the 1930s Depression era. By 1944, however, there were 219 credit unions in Ontario with assets of $4,998,583 and membership totalling 44,840. Van Wezel certainly had other models to study before starting a new one in London and was probably very familiar with the co-op culture of the Netherlands. The first formal meeting to discuss the idea of a credit union was held at the Catholic Culture Centre (now the Colborne Community Centre) on November 14, 1950. About 100 interested people attended and 20 agreed to sign an application for a charter. Roks attended that meeting with his brother Peter and remembers how excited everyone was about the concept of setting up a credit union.

John Strybosch had not moved to Canada at that point, but he understands what motivated people to get involved in those first days: "There were people who had money and could save money and there were people who were in bare need to get some money, to be able to borrow some money so that they could be helped. That was the idea behind all this and that made them study the idea of credit

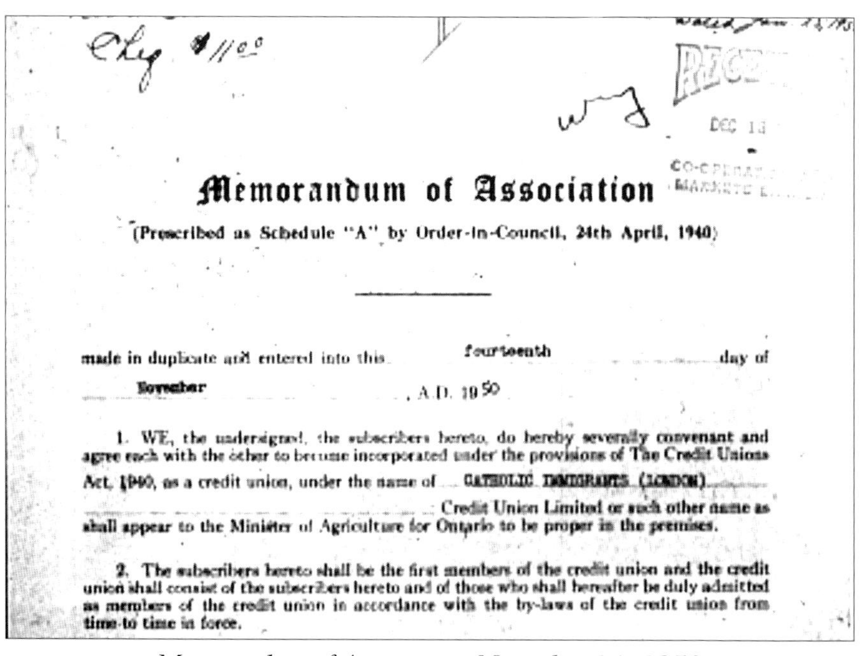

Memorandum of Association

(Prescribed as Schedule "A" by Order-in-Council, 24th April, 1940)

made in duplicate and entered into this fourteenth day of November, A.D. 1950

1. WE, the undersigned, the subscribers hereto, do hereby severally convenant and agree each with the other to become incorporated under the provisions of The Credit Unions Act, 1940, as a credit union, under the name of CATHOLIC IMMIGRANTS (LONDON) Credit Union Limited or such other name as shall appear to the Minister of Agriculture for Ontario to be proper in the premises.

2. The subscribers hereto shall be the first members of the credit union and the credit union shall consist of the subscribers hereto and of those who shall hereafter be duly admitted as members of the credit union in accordance with the by-laws of the credit union from time to time in force.

Memorandum of Association, November 14, 1950

EXCERPTS FROM THE ORIGINAL MEMBERSHIP BYLAW, APPROVED AUGUST 2, 1951

Under Article II

Sec. 1: Membership to the credit union shall be limited to persons who are Dutch/Flemish members of the Catholic Immigration Council of the Diocese of London, Ontario. Members of their immediate families and associations composed of such.

Sec. 2: Application for membership shall be made in writing... and shall bear the approval of a member (of the Board of Directors) and be presented by such member at a regular or special meeting (of the Board) for its approval provided that no such member shall present the name of a person whom he cannot recommend as being honest, industrious and of good habits.

Sec. 3: ...the person whose application has been approved shall not become a member until he has qualified by paying the entrance fee of 25 cents...

Sec. 4: ...a person under the age of twenty-one years may be admitted as a member of the credit union in the same manner as persons over the age of 21...

Under Article III

Sec. 1: The value of each share of the credit union shall be $5.00 (not to exceed $10.00)

unions which were in existence here. There might be a way of combining these people into a group, to help them start. That is basically the idea of the credit union... People had brought in money and did not know where to hide it. So Father spoke of the organization. He got together something like $40,000 before the credit union started working."

A Certificate of Incorporation was issued by the Ontario Minister of Agriculture on January 25, 1951 to officially create what was then known as the Dutch Catholic Immigrants (London) Credit Union Limited. The government would be busy that year as 55 new credit unions were chartered in the first six months of 1951. Unbeknownst to provincial officials, who weren't clear on the definition of "diocese", this particular credit union covered nine different counties in Southwestern Ontario from Windsor and Sarnia to Woodstock and Stratford. A credit union serving that geographic area was unprecedented. Most credit unions of the day served company employees, a union shop, or a single parish. Oddly enough, Ted Smeenk recalls that some people criticized Father van Wezel for not succeeding in making the credit union even larger. Apparently, he had tried to do so because there were Dutch immigrants who lived outside the border of the diocese and yet were interested in joining. Given the smallness of credit unions in the 1950s, it was something of a miracle that the one created by Father van Wezel covered as wide a territory as it did.

There seemed to be plenty of money available from day one, yet the credit union couldn't function forever with Father van Wezel collecting people's dollars and taking them to a bank. Records needed to be kept of all transactions, and loans had to be made to generate interest income for the new credit union. Van Wezel sought out Ted Smeenk, a young Dutchman back in the Netherlands, who had a background in business. Smeenk had heard from his uncle, who was already living in London, that there were tremendous opportunities in Canada. He had been an accountant and office manager for an oil import and export company and later started a radio and appliance business. Smeenk remembers having to apply for 32 permits for his business just to please some Dutch government officials. Even years later, he shakes his head at the amount of bureaucracy the Dutch faced at home in those postwar years. It was time to move.

May 1951: The Smeenk family just before leaving for Canada

First "office" of Credit Union on Adelaide Street

"My wife Pauline, our three children and I emigrated to Canada in May 1951. Reverend Father Jan van Wezel sponsored us because he could use my accounting expertise to help set up the credit union for Dutch and Flemish immigrants. In those days only farmers and tradespeople were allowed into Canada... I had my passport occupation listed as 'electrician', one of the trades allowed into Canada. After all, in my electrical appliance business, I had done some simple electrical installations. Father had applied for a charter with a random collection of newly-arrived immigrants, mostly farmers, as a skeleton board of directors. However, he didn't consider any one of them sufficiently qualified to set up, organize, and manage the credit union. That is what he needed me for. The timing was ideal."

Smeenk got a job as a production worker at Kellogg's and in the evenings worked as secretary/treasurer of the new credit union. He and his family rented an apartment in a house on Adelaide Street in

June of 1951, and here he conducted credit union business initially, despite the protests of his landlady. "This was the first office of the credit union. As soon as I came home, Father van Wezel would be there and we had to go hither and thither to conduct business, meet immigration officials, attend meetings, and visit board members. The work was 'pro-Deo' and for the good of the immigrants. It had to be done after a full day's or night's exhausting work in the factory." Smeenk went with van Wezel to the bank, where members' money was held, and made the necessary arrangements to take over responsibility for managing it. People would show up at Smeenk's doorstep with money, he would provide a written receipt, and then deposit it.

Smeenk encountered some early animosity between the Dutch who had lived in the south and were farmers, and Dutch from the north where he had lived. The farmers believed they were much harder workers than Smeenk was. As well, since he had once been a government employee in the old country, he might have taken some getting used to by the farmers who were wary of bureaucrats. But Smeenk always saw his work as manager as a feather in his cap, something that would serve him well in future jobs. Besides, most people didn't say "No" to a priest back then.

The young credit union was prospering despite not having a proper office. The Smeenks eventually grew uncomfortable in the Adelaide Street premises, and bought a rundown house on Dundas Street with a personal loan of $1,875 from the credit union. Father van Wezel helped them move in the fall of 1951, and came back every day to make calls after Smeenk had finished work at the factory.

When John Strybosch came to Canada in 1951, he also got involved with the credit union almost immediately. "In July, I landed and Father started talking with me right away about the credit union because people had told him I had already been on the board of a credit union. Father had to search to find people who would be willing to serve on the various committees. So we needed 11 people and in the meantime, he visited people and said that we were going to do this and we were going to do that. So we had set up this new Board, credit committee, and supervisory committee. Beautiful really, when you think about it, how we began.

"It started in London, but the distance for people was a problem in this large environment. So then we came up with the idea to set up branches. The branches were absolutely not known in the credit union situation, but we called them 'collectors'. The first one was in

Second office and home at 1229 Dundas Street

September 1951 in Sarnia. Then there was one in Woodstock and on the 22nd of November, one was in Strathroy.

"This was where I was elected in the group with two other people. I was 28, Arie [Adrian] Groot was 29, and Chris Van Loon was 26. They said, 'Well John, you do the administration and collect the money and talk to the people and you do all this.' That's how it started."

The earliest minutes of a Board meeting found in the St. Willibrord archives were dated July 24, 1951. Despite anecdotal evidence that some $40,000 had been collected to start the credit union, minutes from that date show St. Willibrord had 19 members with share balances of $14,508.09. But the credit union was growing quickly. By the time the Board met again on September 20, there were 36 members with more than $26,000 in share balances. By the end of the year, the credit union had $62,183 in assets and 231 members. Business must have been busy enough because the Board asked Smeenk to change his telephone number which was too similar to a local cab company.

The Board initially met in a building at 1295 Dundas Street, not far from the present location of the East London Branch. By 1952, the credit union had opened offices at 100 Central Avenue. Collection points outside London weren't the modern branch buildings you find now. Strybosch, Van Loon, and others worked out of their houses. In some cases, the early "branch offices" were church basements, schools, even someone's garage.

Members would come with their money perhaps once every week or two, on weekends, evenings, or whenever fit their schedule. They would hand over their hard-earned cash, a note would be made of it in a record book, and the money would then be taken to London. The credit union didn't have the resources to give out big loans that are commonplace today. In the early days, people needed money for small appliances, farm equipment, or possibly a car. Large farm loans and mortgages would come later.

Van Loon says the credit union proved popular from the start because the Dutch were used to co-ops back in the Netherlands and in Canada, credit unions were the closest approximation of that system. But not everyone signed up. Some people weren't comfortable with the idea of neighbours

CHOOSING A NEW NAME

In November 1951, the idea of a new name for the credit union was first discussed. The Board selected St. Willibrord after the patron saint of the Netherlands. The original "Dutch Catholic Immigrants (London) Credit Union Limited" was considered too long and unwieldy and difficult to fit on a cheque. The Board accepted the more manageable St. Willibrord unanimously, but according to records, the name wasn't officially recognized until March 7, 1953. Other sources say it was February 15, 1953. As popular as the name St. Willibrord was, there would be several discussions over succeeding years about changing it. In late 1982, the board considered various other options, but decided on St. Willibrord Community Credit Union. After serving so well for almost 50 years, "St. Willibrord" seems firmly established today.

DATE	SHARES RECEIVED	SHARES WITHDRAWN	SHARES BALANCE	DEPOSITS Shares RECEIVED	DEPOSITS WITHDRAWN	BALANCE	TELLER
7.6.52				5 -		5 -	RB
14-3-'53				130 -		135	[illegible]
11-4-'53				50 99		185 99	B
13-4-'53					0 15	185 84	B
6-6-53				47 08		232 92	B
29-6-53					225 00	7 92	B
1-8-53				137 02		144 94	RB
8-6-53	Exch.				0 30	144 64	RB
4-8-53					0 30	144 34	RB
21-7-53	Div.			0 02		144 36	RB
25-9-53				115 52		259 88	RB
28-9-53					254 -	5 88	RB
23-10-53				173 97		179 85	RB

DATE	LOANS LOANED	LOANS REPAID	LOANS BALANCE	CHARGES INTEREST	CHARGES FINES
7.6.52					
13-7-55	1980 -		1980 -		
26-8-55	20 -		2000 -		
7-4-56			2000 -	81 67	
27-7-56		600 -	1400 -	70 -	
30-1-57			1400 -	49 -	
30-7-57		600 -	800 -	49 -	
17-10-57				9 38	
17-10-57	1,100 -		1,900 -		
30-10-57		35 -	1,865 -	5 65	
30-11-57		35 -	1,830 -	5 65	
2-12-57		1,000 -	830 -	10 69	
31-12-57		35 -	795 -	2 53	

Passbook pages from 1952-57

knowing about their finances, how much they were borrowing to buy a car or a freezer, and how long it was taking to pay the money back. Even though banks didn't do a lot of consumer lending, going to a Canadian bank was an option that some Dutch Catholics did pursue. They were, however, certainly missing a more friendly, sociable way of handling their money.

John Féron, who was a collector in the 50s, remembers the folksy meetings with members at "the kitchen table, Sunday morning after Mass. They would bring in $50 or $20 or $100 or whatever it was. The 'collector' would then take that in. It was all done in a very simple way. There was a lot of trust. A lot of trust. I can honestly say I cannot remember ever mistrusting any of the collectors."

Strybosch adds, "They were all strangers in a strange country and they didn't trust anyone beyond, but my family and I had a very good reputation, and that helped. They always say that groups of people, by instinct, look for a leader and this person usually has characteristics that make him a leader for some reason. I think that is the best explanation. There was an enormous trust. It was unbelievable."

In those early days, bringing money to deposit with the collectors wasn't just a business transaction, it was also a social time. Dutch was, of course, the language of communication back then, and even formal Board meetings didn't adopt English as the official language until 1961. Whatever might not have been discussed after church on Sunday mornings could be hashed out at the collectors' houses. Strybosch smiles and looks at his wife Lena when he recalls those visits, "Oh, the pies, and gallons and gallons of coffee you have made."

Adds Lena, "In the winter they would come together in the dining room to talk with John, and I would be in the kitchen with the kids. Farmers would come in. They visited. The house was full of people always."

In March 1952, Smeenk was joined at the credit union by a young woman of 23 who had come to Canada from the Netherlands the year before. Frederica Vanbrock (née Beretta) came to work at the credit union as its secretary. She had experience back home in the export business and a childhood spent in the country gave her some familiarity with farmers' concerns. She could speak English but had something of a rude awakening when she first arrived and went to church in Strathroy. "There was an elderly Irish priest who had such a brogue. I talked to my sister after we walked out of church and said, 'I didn't understand a word.' I was so disappointed. But then a Canadian lady behind me tapped me on the shoulder and said, 'Darling, I have been going here for 40 years and I still don't understand him.'"

Vanbrock recalls attending many meetings in those early years in different parts of Southwestern Ontario to accommodate the rural members. She would keep records of transactions and was often responsible for taking care of the money until it could be safely deposited. "It was an opportunity for people to bring money and learn about the credit union. I went home many times with I don't know how many thousands of dollars in my little purse. I had been bonded very quickly. The next day I would walk to the bank, since I had no car, and deposit the money."

Vanbrock took on other responsibilities over the next five years at the credit union, and from approximately June to October 1952, she was essentially in charge of running the operation. This happened because Smeenk had taken a job with an insurance company, and some members, concerned that his new job of selling insurance was in conflict with running the affairs of the credit union, suggested he resign. Smeenk was upset with the hard feelings created and eventually left his St. Willibrord job, though he remained a member for many years afterward. Until Gus Cammaert took on the job of office manager/treasurer in October, Vanbrock handled the day-to-day business, learning more about finances and loans. The credit union kept strict records and issued receipts. But there was always that personal touch, so much so that Vanbrock could recall the membership numbers of more than 1,000 people by the time she left her job. "When people tell you all about their financial situation, you become a part of their lives and you take that very seriously."

The credit committee, set up under Siebert Graat, was responsible for deciding who got loans and for how much. Vanbrock was the administrator who recorded the transactions. Credit

Siebert Graat
Board President
1951-59

committee members met with members who wanted loans, discussed what collateral was available, and the character of the person applying for the money. She recalls few bad loans in those early years and notes how flexible payments were arranged around the time the farmers had crops and money coming in. While the credit union was set up to help Dutch immigrants get a start, not everyone who asked for money received a loan. In fact, earlier guidelines from November 1951, indicate that to a get a loan, a member had to have been a consistent saver for at least three consecutive months.

The credit committee didn't just hand out money at will. It had to be sure that the person asking for money was a good risk because it was other members' money that was being used. "Everyone was so conscientious that it was everybody else's money," says Vanbrock. "You don't think of that when you go to a bank, but we protected the money."

Vanbrock believes there was another benefit to helping all these newcomers get started. She recalls a time when a government inspector came for a visit to check out the credit union's balance sheets and ensure everything was in order. He wanted to see some of the farms that were being helped by the credit union, and went on a tour of the region. She notes how impressed he was that properties abandoned several years before were now in the hands of hard-working people trying to make the land prosperous. "Lots of farms had been left by younger generations. The government was impressed that older farms and houses were occupied by big families where all the kids worked. It really did the country a lot of good."

By the end of March 1952, van Wezel had been transferred to Ottawa to help Dutch immigrants there (Father J.J. Karskens took over as spiritual adviser for several months and then was succeeded by Father Martin Grootscholten), but the credit union, though still young, was up and running and functioning smoothly. Cammaert, who was paid $250 a month, had co-op and loan experience and provided the kind of leadership needed. Vanbrock remembers him as being "great with the people, and an absolutely wonderful man" who understood farmers' concerns.

Another key figure involved in the credit union in those early days was Bill Intven. He had emigrated from the Netherlands in

William Intven
Board President
1959-70

1950, leaving behind a good job as head of the municipal department of public works, and settled in the St. Thomas area. He missed the first historic meeting in November, but was aware a credit union was being formed. Early on, he became a member of the supervisory committee. "I was in there for a year or two. Then, about three years later, I was elected to the Board. I was secretary twice. As soon as I was on the Board, they made me secretary which I liked better than president." Intven served on the Board for more than 35 years, was president throughout the1960s, and a key figure in making English the official language of meetings in 1961. "If you want to keep living in this country, you'd better talk the language. Because you can't do business, or have very much social contact with the rest of the population. So it's absolutely the very, very first demand that you speak the language. A lot of Dutch people didn't know any English when they came here. But there was no objection [to making English the official language], although it took a long while before they were as comfortable with English as they were with Dutch."

By early 1953, the credit union was an important part of the Dutch-Catholic community of Southwestern Ontario. There were some 600 members, and these people who put their faith in the credit union helped make it successful in the beginning years. One early member was Matt van Gelueken, who joined the credit union in 1953, and helped build the safe in the new headquarters at 150 Kent St. where the credit union relocated in October of that year. He remembers the general layout of the Kent Street office, how the room where the safe was built was in the small office on the left as one entered the building, and how Father Grootscholten's office was on the right.

It was no longer wise to leave all paperwork related to running the credit union lying on shelves in the small office. Staff were not particularly worried about theft, but were very concerned about fire. A concrete safe was needed to secure the papers, documents, and whatever money was in the office at any given time. With this improved security, members knew their money and records were in good hands.

At this time, the city members were more likely to be savers and, by all accounts, didn't mind that their money was being used for loans by many rural members who needed capital to start farms and buy equipment. The Dutch immigrants who came here brought their cooperative sense with them and planted it into a Canadian society that was prospering.

As Frederica Vanbrock says, "Dutch people are very trustworthy, hard-working and honest. They will not give up and they'll support each other. In the beginning, Dutch people had big families with lots of children. Girls would go out to work when they were old enough, and boys would farm or work in factories. All that money was put together. The way the Dutch immigrants operated worked. It also benefited the credit union, of course."

The credit union continued to prosper throughout the 1950s by increasing its membership and expanding the range of services.

THE NEW VAULT

Father Martin Grootscholten, spiritual adviser to the credit union, probably designed the new vault built at the Kent Street office in 1953. Volunteers gathered to perform the labour, and the credit union bought the materials.

Before the vault could be constructed, footings and supporting pillars were erected in the basement to support the weight of all the concrete and the steel door which was manufactured especially for the safe. Matt van Gelueken, now a semi-retired dairy farmer living north of London, was among the people who worked on the footings and the brick pillars. When these were in place, workers started pouring the walls for the safe. All concrete was mixed with hand tools, and work was undertaken whenever members and friends had free time, usually in the evenings and on Saturdays.

Siebert Graat had a body shop in East London at the time, and he made the steel door which had a combination lock. Van Gelueken estimates the size of the interior at about four feet wide, eight to ten feet deep, and six feet high. Electricity was supplied to the interior of the safe for a light. Walls were about a foot thick and there was a concrete floor and ceiling. It took two weeks of part-time labour to construct the vault.

The door was made from quarter-inch steel and extremely heavy. It took considerable manpower to hang the door, and special half-inch tempered steel drill bits were brought from Graat's Body Shop to drill holes through the plates to anchor the hinges in the concrete. "We shorted out a couple of drills in the process. They just could not take the pressure we put on them." The door had been designed so that when it was locked, bolts would shoot through both sides of the door into the concrete walls.

FATHER JAN VAN WEZEL

Father Jan van Wezel or "Father John", as some called him, was born on September 7, 1908, in Middelburg, the Netherlands, a town not far from the North Sea. He became a member of the Congregation of the Priests of the Sacred Heart almost nineteen years to the day on September 8, 1927. Van Wezel was ordained on June 29, 1936 in Innsbruck, Austria, and from 1937 to 1945 was a chaplain and later director of the Apostleship of the Sea (the International Union of Catholic Seafarers) in Rotterdam. From 1945 to 1949, van Wezel was assigned by the Ministry of Justice as head chaplain for the prisoners of war in the Netherlands.

Father Jan van Wezel

That he was used to helping his fellow humans was not out of the ordinary; it was what priests did. And whatever fervour burned inside him to help others certainly benefited those Dutch immigrants who found themselves in Canada in the early 1950s. In his role as Associate Director of Immigration for the Roman Catholic Diocese, van Wezel was often the first person they met, the first new person they came to trust, and someone who often became their financial adviser. For him, the "Parish" embraced all Dutch Catholic immigrants in London, and the surrounding areas.

Frederica Vanbrock remembers him as a man with "tremendous influence. People had total trust in him. He was the one who knew the system of the credit union, who really understood the possibilities, and he was the one who went to bat to get our charter organized."

Others agreed that his status in the Dutch-Canadian community of Southwestern Ontario was supreme. Dutch priests wielded great authority in the Netherlands in those days and it was much the same in Canada at that time. What van Wezel wanted he usually got, but that influence was certainly tempered by his knowledge and ability to help others. "He was extremely conscientious, very business-like, a pure economist," Vanbrock recalls. "I think he had studied economics because he knew about business. He was absolutely dedicated to doing things for people who were in a totally new environment. Many of them didn't speak the language."

In 1952, van Wezel founded and became a member of the Canadian Netherlands Immigration Council. He also founded the Central Bureau for the Netherlands Catholic Immigration in

Ottawa, where he had been transferred that same year.

From 1958 to 1974, van Wezel served as priest in various Ontario parishes, as hospital chaplain in the Diocese of Hamilton, and on several committees. His considerable work was recognized in 1972 when Queen Juliana of the Netherlands honoured him with the Royal Order "Ridder in de Orde van Oranje Nassau" (Companion of the Order of Orange Nassau) at a ceremony in Toronto. Although it's unclear whether the following incident happened at this point or with another member of royalty, Bill Intven recalls van Wezel's sense of humour. Apparently, he said something to a royal family member that made her laugh. "And when I asked Father what he said, he told me he said to her in Dutch, 'Would you like to use the confessional for a while?'"

In 1979, and in failing health, van Wezel was given permission to return to the Netherlands. He lived a quiet life there but, by 1986, he had been diagnosed with lung cancer. Father Jan van Wezel died in St. Elizabeth Hospital in Tilburg, Netherlands, on March 27, 1987. He was buried in the cemetery of the Priests of the Sacred Heart at Asten in the southern Netherlands. He had touched the lives of many during his career and, through his dedication and hard work in the early 1950s, created a credit union that today is healthy, strong, and still growing.

At the end of the 50s, there were 2,000 plus members with more than $734,000 in assets. Though Vanbrock left the credit union in 1957 when she married and moved to California, she has admired the growth of St. Willibrord from afar and is grateful for the experience it gave her. "I have nothing but wonderful memories of those years. I knew the credit union had tremendous potential. I think I had enough business foresight to know that it could grow with the right leadership, strong leadership to make the necessary moves. I always knew that the dedication of people would create the potential for something good."

As with any new organization, there would be growing pains and struggles before St. Willibrord Community Credit Union would turn that tremendous potential into long-lasting success. But real growth had begun, thanks to the ingenuity, hard work, and faith of so many early members.

AT THE TIME

Newspaper headlines reported a double murder-suicide in a small Southwestern Ontario town, a plane crash in the French Alps, war raging halfway around the world, and talk of economic union in Europe.

But this wasn't a newspaper from today; it was coverage of news in *The London Free Press* on November 14, 1950, the day that about 100 people came together to discuss the formation of a credit union for Dutch Catholic immigrants.

Although there's no arguing that much has changed since that important day some 50 years ago, a snapshot of life on that Tuesday had items that seem oddly familiar to modern readers. For example, a vice-consul of the Netherlands speaking to a group in Toronto said the Benelux union (Belgium, Netherlands and Luxembourg) was proceeding so well he expected that the rest of Western Europe would unite in the near future.

The Korean War was at a standstill that day because of sub-freezing temperatures, although American troops later captured a town with little resistance. People were in shock because of an airplane crash in France that killed all 58 Canadian passengers who had just come from a visit with the Pope in Rome, while closer to home a triple slaying in Walkerton, Ontario, had police and others shaking their heads over the tragedy.

But a further look in the paper gives us glimpses into a London way of life that has indeed changed over the years. A package of Sweet Caps cigarettes was selling for 45 cents, while an ad from Kellogg's was trumpeting its newest cereal — Raisin Bran. Canadian money was being accepted at par at Detroit's Hotel Wolverine, while Gurd's Sports Shop on Dundas Street was selling the latest Kodak cameras for $14.95 and up.

The movie *My Blue Heaven*, starring Betty Grable and Dan Dailey, was playing at the Capitol while the Palace had *Under Capricorn*, a Hitchcock movie starring Ingrid Bergman and Joseph Cotten (admission was 38 cents, tax included). At the Grand Theatre that evening, the International Grand Opera Company of New York was performing *Carmen* with a top admission price of $3.45.

And speaking of New York, a news item reported people in that city were flocking to see a new documentary *You Can Beat the A-Bomb* which explained precautions to be taken "if and when an A-Bomb drops."

Prime Minister Louis St. Laurent was

expected to shuffle his cabinet before the year was out, and the government announced a plan to spend $1 billion on arms to build up the country's defence.

The London Jaycees were launching a campaign to get housewives to vote early in the December 4 municipal election. In the past, most women had waited for their husbands to return home from work before voting and this had caused congestion at the polls in the late afternoon and early evening hours.

In sports, the Western Mustangs were getting ready for a sudden-death playoff game against the McGill Redmen, and New York Yankees pitcher Whitey Ford was ordered to report for induction into the army. The Winnipeg Blue Bombers beat the Edmonton Eskimos to win the right to represent the West in the Grey Cup, and the Toronto Maple Leafs were in first place in the NHL standings.

TV listings for the day only had information on American stations as there were no Canadian channels in existence. Featured programs included *Buck Rogers*, *The Amateur Hour*, and *Fireside Theatre*. CBS in New York had set up a display in a Fifth Avenue showroom to demonstrate to the public its latest innovation — colour television.

Radio was still popular, and shows such as *Bob Hope* and *Fibber McGee and Molly* were among the selections for that evening. CFPL Radio was broadcasting *Symphony Hour* and *Search for Talent* while the CBC had *Canadian Cavalcade*.

The comics pages featured Donald Duck, Superman, Alley Oop, Red Ryder and Bugs Bunny, while a business editor for Canadian Press was expressing his surprise at a unique group of women who had actually become successful members of The Canadian Exporters Association.

A Blenheim, Ontario, farmer won the hay championship at the Royal Winter Fair in Toronto, and hothouse tomatoes were selling for 25 cents a pound at the Covent Garden Market. There were plenty of jobs for bowling pin boys, stenographers, telephone operators, and service station attendants, advertised in the paper.

Roots &
Branches

Cultivating an Organization

CHAPTER 3

An organization is only as effective and successful as the people who run it. Strong management with a clear vision for the future is as beneficial to a group as ineffectual management is detrimental. St. Willibrord is no different from other enterprises in that it has had, at different times, strong, well-directed management, and management whose talents were perhaps not suited to its needs and goals. And, as in any other organization, most who served at the helm of the credit union brought different skills, abilities, and personalities to the role.

What seems to have defined successful leaders at St. Willibrord, more than any single characteristic, has been their loyalty to the original idea presented by credit union founders, pride in their work, and a close association with the membership. Time and again, people interviewed for this book mentioned individuals who were actively involved with St. Willibrord, on a part-time basis, and noted that they often didn't need the stipend associated with the work since their income from farming or other business interests would have been sufficient. But these members served because they believed in the credit union concept, and in St. Willibrord in particular.

It was also noted that, later on, those in leadership positions might have been tempted by more lucrative offers of employment from other institutions, but turned them down in favour of remaining with St. Willibrord. The sense of belonging to something that was gaining momentum and popularity, and demonstrated a philosophy of

Ted Smeenk
Manager:
1951-52

Frederica Vanbrock
Manager:
1952

August Cammaert
Manager:
1952-57 and 1963-66

helping individuals achieve financial independence, is usually credited with keeping effective management at St. Willibrord.

Now and then, there were conflicts among some of those who directed the course of the credit union, but these clashes of personality were remarkably few and far between. The good of the credit union and its membership seems to have continuously outweighed personal differences.

From the beginning, St. Willibrord enjoyed leadership which was strong and devoted to the continued success and growth of the operation. The first person to hold the position of manager, or secretary/treasurer as it was called at the time, was Ted Smeenk. Following Smeenk's tenure, St. Willibrord took what was an unusual step in the early 1950s by appointing a woman as interim manager. Frederica Vanbrock served in that capacity for five months in 1952, before Gus Cammaert took over the responsibilty. By all reports, Ms. Vanbrock was a knowledgeable and effective manager who did much to organize the credit union and establish the attitude of thoroughness and efficiency that would carry it through the formative years.

Cammaert served from 1952 until 1957, followed by Nico van Wijk. After van Wijk left the organization, Cammaert returned and stayed at St. Willibrord until his untimely death in 1966 at the age of 56. Martin Verbeek was manager from 1966 to 1968, and following the departure of Verbeek, John Strybosch became general manager, a position he held until 1988 when the current president and chief executive officer, Jack Smit, accepted the position.

Before stepping into his role as general manager Strybosch, like

Nicolaas van Wijk
Manager:
1957-63

Martin Verbeek
Manager:
1966-68

John Strybosch
General Manager:
1969-88

some of the other early managers, had held several positions in the credit union, one of which was cashier/collector in the Strathroy district. Initially, the position of collector was a volunteer one, gradually changing to one paying around $75 a week. Taking care of deposits though was not the only task entrusted to the staff. Since the credit union's beginnings, members had joined in order to have two basic benefits: a secure place to put their money and a source for reasonably-priced personal and business loans. Securing the deposits was never a major problem, but delivering and servicing loans was more complicated.

Jack Smit
President & CEO:
1988 to present

Lending Activities

During the credit union's early development, newcomers were still arriving from the Netherlands, and regulations on how much money they could bring with them slowly relaxed. As a consequence, the capital available was growing. In 1955, based on the strength of that growth, Gus Cammaert was partly responsible for approaching the Farmers' Lending Bank in the Netherlands on behalf of the credit union to secure a loan of $100,000. This allowed them to give larger loans for longer periods of time to farmers and businesses, and to support the more risky second mortgages. The Ontario Credit Union League, now Credit Union Central, was not in a position to finance these larger loans. It was seen as a significant vote of confidence in St. Willibrord Community Credit Union when the Boerenleenbank made the loan to the local organization.

By 1960, the net profit of the company was $13,325.41, which was down from the previous year when it was $16,078.78. Assets were up though, and shares were greater. In 1961, the credit committee chairman, Harry Willems, would observe that the credit union could look back on 1960 as a year that had seen loan activity as never before. Membership increased by 335 people, or almost a new member each day. In 1962, he noted in the annual report that higher demand for sufficient credit meant "our credit union remains an excellent source of help to establish members in their settlement and businesses." Although people were requesting money for farms, houses, and cars, most applications were for working capital.

As chair of the credit committee in 1964, Willems noted that there was a decline in applications for farm machinery, car, and truck loans. One reason was that other financial institutions had entered this field of financing. But he felt that perhaps members did not realize they were paying out unreasonable amounts of interest by going outside the credit union. So his committee recommended that broader information be given out to members about the services offered, and especially about the comparatively lower loan interest rates.

In his 1967 report to members, Board president William Intven said loan activity was hampered by a money scarcity in North America. He asked for a more cooperative spirit especially from members who had benefited from credit union loans in the past and who now had surplus funds. "Could there be a more worthwhile credit union Centennial goal than accelerating our spirit of cooperation to the extent that all legitimate loans needed by our members could be provided by our members?"

An investigation by the Department of Financial and Commercial Affairs of the Ontario Government into the operations of the credit union in 1968 had been sparked by the fact that St. Willibrord was issuing loans over the approved limit set by the government. "We had approached the government several times to have the limit expanded," recalls Strybosch, "but it was not granted." Then, several members of the St. Willibrord management team visited Niagara Credit Union in Virgil, Ontario, because that credit union was issuing loans of up to $30,000 to its members, a figure well above the $5,000 limit St. Willibrord was able to offer. "We asked them how they had managed to reach this level of loans," says Strybosch. They were told that each time the provincial government came to inspect them, the inspectors raised the loan limit to match what the credit union was already issuing. "But the manager warned us that we must have our house in order if we were to increase our loans as well. We asked Verbeek if our house was in order, and he said it was, but when the inspectors came, they found it was not so." They noted a discrepancy in the records of the Sarnia branch and Martin Verbeek, as manager, was held to account. Shortly after, J. Turley, Director of Field Services for the Ontario Credit Union League, came to a meeting and was asked to do an analysis of procedures at the credit union. Following this request, Verbeek resigned his position. It should be noted that, in the end, the credit union suffered no financial loss related to this incident, and there were no ongoing ill effects as a result of the investigation into raising loan limits. In fact, within the next few years, they were able to offer larger loans.

Early on, one of the challenges faced by people responsible for day-to-day operations of the credit union was collecting delinquent loans. In his role as fieldman for the credit union, Strybosch learned what happened to people who, for one reason or another, were unable to repay their loans. "In that position, I had to organize and control the local collectors, make contact with them, set up meetings, and explain how to handle the money and loans. But it was also part of my duties to go after delinquent loans." No doubt some hard feelings grew out of the fact that, on occasion, people were unable or unwilling to repay what they owed.

There were not a lot of these delinquent loans but, according to past records, there were some. By 1954, the bylaws stated that no loans larger than $200 should be made without security, no loan for more than a $1,000 in excess of unencumbered savings, and that no loan should exceed $4,000 without a secured first mortgage on real estate, and $2,000 on a second mortgage. The financial records of the credit union show occasional lapses in payment and forfeitures of property for unpaid loans. The sums of monies lost were rarely substantial, but loans amounting to between $500 and $2,000 were occasionally forfeited. Records show that the credit union tried hard to recover unpaid loans, but in a few instances, the effort was not successful as people owing the money had vanished. A letter from W.M. Jaffray, director of the Department of the Attorney General in Toronto, to E.J. Hutchinson at the Credit Union in June of 1965, lists a number of defaulted loans, overdrafts and bankruptcies. The list makes it clear that there were occasions when people simply could not repay loans, and either defaulted, or in a few cases, disappeared.

CHANGING MEMBERSHIP

When St. Willibrord was first created in 1951, it went under the rather unwieldy name of "The Dutch Catholic Immigrants (London) Credit Union Limited" (DCI(L)CU). The Ontario Gazette, Volume LXXXVI, dated Toronto, March 7, 1953, and with reference to the Credit Unions Act, acknowledges the name change of the fledgling credit union to the more familiar St. Willibrord (London) Credit Union Limited.

No sooner was the credit union established, than letters began arriving from the Credit Union League in Toronto welcoming the establishment of what was still DCI(L)CU, inviting the organization to join. One letter dated February 2, 1951, pointed out that the initial fee for joining the League was $2.00. "When your credit union has been in operation for a year, dues are 50 cents per member per year, with the exception of children under sixteen years of age."

By that July, the credit union was a member in good standing with the League. In December, the League sent a letter to the credit union reminding them to pay the dues of 44 cents per member, adding, "Promptness in paying your 1952 dues will be deeply appreciated, and will enable the League to continue its efforts to expand and develop our great movement." A note was attached informing the new credit union, "Dues for each year are due and payable on January 1 of each year, and a credit union is considered in arrears if dues are not received by March 1." The letter was signed by John M. Halinan, general manager.

Meanwhile, the Department of Insurance of the Ontario government followed the creation of the new credit union with interest, and a letter from the Supervisor of Credit Unions, dated May 8, 1957, recommended that when the bylaws were updated, the bond of membership in the credit union be clarified to include Dutch and Flemish members of the Catholic Immigrant Council of the Roman Catholic Diocese of London, Ontario, including their wives, husbands, and dependants, and for deposit purposes only, "...any unincorporated organization or association of such members."

In July of 1965, an amendment was proposed to "...extend (membership) to Dutch and Flemish immigrants residing within the geographical area of the Roman Catholic Diocese of London, Ontario." This amendment was intended to allow people who were not of Roman Catholic denomination to become members of the credit union.

The amendment was not allowed by the Ontario government and, in a letter to the Supervisor of Credit Unions for the province, general manager A. (Gus) Cammaert explained that the amendment was proposed because "...in these changing times, all that is possible should be done to improve the relations between the different Christian faiths, and as a growing number of Dutch and Flemish immigrants of other than Roman Catholic faith request membership in their particular credit union, the Board of Directors indeed feels that a step in the right direction would made to help improve these relations." Still, this amendment was never passed.

The need to change its terms of defining who could and could not apply to become a member of the credit union was one that would continue to hamper St. Willibrord until the acquisition of Co-op Services Credit Union in 1977. That merger brought a new, already established, group of members into the still predominantly Dutch Catholic credit union. In 1982, membership was extended to "persons who reside or are employed in the counties of Middlesex, and Lambton, to the town of Blenheim and 10 mile radius thereof, and Stratford." No mention is made of religious or cultural affiliations.

Early Services

Many of the first St. Willibrord members had been used to dealing primarily with the Boerenleenbank in the Netherlands, a full-service, well-established banking institution. When Dutch immigrants came to Ontario, they expected St. Willibrord to provide the same full slate of services, but that was not the credit union concept in the 50s and 60s. Even the Credit Union League did not see that the credit unions should be delivering services such as chequing or business lending. There were very few credit unions that delivered these services, and they did so without League support because it did not see this aspect of banking as being part of the credit union vision. In order to offer services such as chequing, St. Willibrord had to deal with a bank as a secondary agent to get cheques cleared.

Consequently, the range of services at St. Willibrord was always wider than other credit unions with the possible exception of the Niagara Credit Union, which also had a large contingent of self-employed people and developed a similar variety of services. St. Willibrord members viewed services like chequing accounts and business loans as basic functions, and the credit union had to deliver. Members wanted to use the credit union as their primary financial institution and, while most credit unions did not see themselves as such, that was considered to be a basic part of St. Willibrord's mandate. Additional financial services such as travellers cheques were being made available to members for the first time in 1964, and plans were in the works to establish a student loan plan by 1965 to help younger members

Credit union head office opens in $80,000 quarters tomorrow

Several years of planning and development will climax tomorrow with the official opening of an $80,000 head office for the St. Willibrord Credit Union Limited...

A staff of six is headed by H. C. Giesen, treasurer and office manager and Jack Varmue, loan manager...

The nucleus of the building fund for the new headquarters was started in 1965.

That fund, together with a debenture issue provided the financial support for this year's building project...

Opening of a new head office at 151 Albert Street on June 26, 1966
*(*The London Free Press *article excerpt reprinted with permission)*

Exterior of Albert Street head office

continue their education after Grade 13. Wherever there was a perceived need, St. Willibrord found a way to deliver the service. That was the case with bookkeeping aid (perhaps a precursor to what has become the financial planning assistance and advice offered by the credit union today), health insurance, and travel planning.

In the late 50s and early 60s, St. Willibrord had arranged charter flights to fly interested members back to the Netherlands as an added service. For a lot of credit union members, this was a highlight in their lives because they had found an affordable way to visit their homeland. For anybody going back for the first time, after being away for 10 or 12 years, these opportunities were real celebrations, and also very emotional. By the mid 60s, cooperative arrangements were in place with other similar Dutch credit unions of Ontario, resulting in the creation of the Dutch Canadian Alliance. This alliance had a dual purpose: providing group life insurance and charter travel arrangements. Credit union staff members acted as informal booking agents for the travel service which actually ran the charters.

Among the factors that brought an end to St. Willibrord's involvement with arranging travel was a combination of changing government regulations, and new trends in charter flights. There was also an increase in the prosperity of St. Willibrord members who were going back to Europe more frequently, booking their own

AT THE TIME

1960s

Wellington Square Mall opens in London in 1960

President John F. Kennedy is assassinated in Dallas, Texas, in 1963

Also in 1963, audio-cassettes overshadow eight-track tapes as the format of choice for music recording

In 1965, a new London Free Press building is constructed on York Street

The first episode of the television show Star Trek appears in 1966 then creates a huge audience and cult following later called "Trekkies"

The first Superbowl is held and televised on June 15, 1967

EXPO 67 World's Fair opens in Montreal as Canada celebrates its Centennial Year

Legendary singer and movie actress Judy Garland (b. 1922) dies in 1969

On August 15, 1969, a folk music and arts festival near Woodstock, New York, grows to become one of the largest open-air music festivals ever held

Richard M. Nixon becomes the 37th President of The United States in 1969

On July 20, 1969, Neil Armstrong, as commander of the Apollo 11 lunar mission, is the first person to set foot on the moon

arrangements through separate travel agencies. In the early years though, unless they arranged the flights at charter rates, a lot of people simply could not afford to go. St. Willibrord took this and other functions as part of its mission, and that eventually led to a review of the credit union's services in the mid-to-late 60s. At that time, the credit union did not have a firm enough structure and management to hold all the service threads together. When John Strybosch became manager, he believed that the credit union had to focus strictly on financial services, and drop the non-core activities such as health insurance and travel bookings.

The pathway to expansion and growth was not always an easy one to navigate for this relatively young organization. The late 50s and early 60s were somewhat turbulent times at St. Willibrord. There were several different managers in succession, and tough decisions had to be made about the range of services which the credit union could realistically offer its members. However, along the way, management and Board members with creative ideas and dedication to co-op principles were able to lead St. Willibrord toward success and further prosperity.

A CHRISTMAS STORY

Joe Beechie was retained as legal adviser to St. Willibrord Community Credit Union from 1955 until he retired in 1990. He recalls when the credit union went out of its way to provide added services.

"Over the years, I performed a variety of fairly routine legal services for St. Willibrord, primarily related to real estate transactions, with very little out of the ordinary. But one event does stand out in my mind. This dates back to the time when St. Willibrord was facilitating trips back to the Netherlands through WIBO Travel Services. In those days, they had what they called 'affinity charters', which meant that in order for a group of people to charter a flight anywhere, they all had to belong to a recognized club of some sort.

There was a charter slated to leave for the Netherlands one Christmas on a KLM flight leaving from the airport in Toronto, now called Pearson. The flight was sold out, when I suddenly received a complaint from the International Transport Association saying that the flight was not a legitimate charter. As it turned out, not all the people on the flight had belonged to St. Willibrord long enough for them to qualify as being part of the 'affinity charter'.

I received the call at about one in the afternoon saying the flight wouldn't be allowed to take off at 11:00 pm. I got on the phone to the Minister of Transport in Ottawa, Jack Pickersgill and told his executive assistant, Ian Fraser, that Mr. Pickersgill might be interested to learn that there were 300 disgruntled Dutch voters sitting at the airport in Toronto, about to have their Christmas visit home cancelled because of some minor, bureaucratic red tape.

To his credit, the assistant called me back within half an hour with the news that the flight was back on, provided I could assure him that all people on the flight were indeed members of St. Willibrord Credit Union. So Bill Intven and I, and a couple of other Board members, rushed down to the airport where I set up a table by the gate and stood, with notary stamp in hand and affidavit forms, getting all the people on the flight to swear they were valid members of St. Willibrord. As people signed the form they got on the plane. That was a close thing. But we made it. I'll never forget that Christmas."

Roots &
Branches

A Change in Climate

CHAPTER 4

There is no doubt that one of the crucial turning points in St. Willibrord's history was that cold, January night in 1969 when John Strybosch drove into London from Arkona and told the Board of Directors he would accept the position of general manager. It would not be too bold to say that the credit union, as it's known today, could pinpoint that event, and the merger with Co-op Services of London eight years later, as the two biggest influences on its modern development. With Strybosch came a more disciplined and business-like approach without losing the personal, almost family-style, atmosphere that set St. Willibrord apart from other financial institutions such as banks and trust companies. And while, in hindsight, turning the reins over to Strybosch at the time was the sensible and logical thing to do, even he wasn't sure the position was right for him.

"We had no manager and we were searching. Incidentally, I had almost decided not to work for the credit union anymore," Strybosch recalls. "I was sick and tired of it in a certain sense. We had the bookkeeping service [in Arkona] which demanded much more, so I decided to concentrate on that." But the Board wanted Strybosch to take on the job. The instability of the mid-to-late 60s, with managers coming and going, needed to be resolved. They had advertised for a new manager and there were some applicants, but something lacking in them led then-president Bill Intven to visit Strybosch.

"It was a very pleasant visit," Strybosch remembers. "We talked about everything. It was about twelve o'clock at night when he said, 'Won't you take on the management of St. Willibrord?' Now this is something I had thought of before, even years before. Sometimes it appealed to me and sometimes not. Even with all the troubles we had and disappointments we had to overcome, it kind of appealed to me. My heart was always in the credit union, really. It still is. I said, 'Bill, I don't know.' Well, he said, 'A week from now we're having a Board meeting. Would you know by then?'"

Strybosch promised him an answer and spent the next few days pondering the offer. His life and business were in Arkona, and he wasn't sure he wanted to uproot his family and move to London. Peter Van Engelen, in Forest, was a big booster of Strybosch becoming manager and tried to talk him into it. But even on the day of the meeting, Strybosch still wasn't sure what to do. "The evening came that we went to the Board meeting. My wife Lena asked, 'What will you do now? What are you going to say tonight?' I said, 'I really don't know. I'm fifty-fifty.'"

Peter Van Engelen
Board Member
1963-70

He and Van Engelen drove to the meeting that night. They don't recall their exact words, but they did discuss the decision. Strybosch was 45 years old. He had a successful career, and now he was being offered the chance to take over a credit union that had gone through some rocky times in recent years. If there was a particular factor that swayed Strybosch's mind that night, it's been lost in the haze of time. But when he arrived, his mind was made up. Strybosch picks up the story: "Bill Intven was waiting at the door. When I walked in he said, 'What did you decide John?' I said, 'I'll take it.'" Intven took Strybosch down to the basement where the Board was meeting and introduced him as the new manager of St. Willibrord. In February, 1969, Strybosch, with an annual salary of $12,000, officially took over. Things would definitely be different from then on.

Strybosch made it clear from the beginning that he wanted to run the show, and it seems that there was little resistance from anyone because of the problems the credit union had had in the previous few years. Once they knew Strybosch was on board, even the government backed off any investigating they were doing. "I said to the Board that we were in a horrible mess and I want freedom," Strybosch says. "I don't want interfering from the Board. No B.S."

As Strybosch settled into his new office on Albert Street, he recognized several problems which needed to be cleared up quickly. There were about 35 loans not in order, and some credit union employees had the kind of less-than-positive morale one might expect after enduring a series of managers in a short space of time. People were taking money and putting IOUs in the cashbox, while member deposits were handled so slowly it took as many as 20 days to record them in the books. St. Willibrord members seemed to be easygoing about this and accepted practices they wouldn't put up with today. Strybosch remembers, with a laugh, one woman on staff who looked at him when he started and said, "Well, you're joker number five," referring to the bosses she'd had to deal with. But this "joker" was different. When she asked him for a raise, he didn't budge. She quit. Strybosch was glad to be able to start fresh with someone new.

He didn't think administrative staff were hard-working enough, took too many coffee breaks, and needed to better understand that members' needs should be dealt with quickly and efficiently. He wanted employees who would help build the credit union business and be as professional as possible when serving members. "I wanted to set up a system that was well-operated, well-oiled, you know, with several branches and then try to expand the business in Southwestern Ontario. That was the vision."

It might be what we now call empire-building, with Strybosch as emperor. But this "emperor" was something of a benevolent one. He certainly knew all the players and many of the members at the credit union, understood the organization from the inside out, and wasn't afraid to dish out fatherly advice or hire young staff he could mold to his vision.

Early on, Strybosch hired two people who would help meet his goals. The first was a young woman, Ans Vandenberg, who arrived from the Netherlands in 1969. She had office experience and was quick to note that the credit union needed a change. "She was a good lady, God's gift," Strybosch says. "She was here a week and asked, 'How long has this business been disorganized?' I said, 'It's not only disorganized, it's more like a manure pile.'"

In May 1969, another key employee came on board, Jack Smit, the man who would eventually succeed Strybosch as manager. He too had arrived from the Netherlands and was looking for work. Starting as a teller, he handled a variety of administrative tasks. Despite being something of a rebel in those days, he also recognized the need to make St. Willibrord more business-like. "Things were messy at the credit union then," Smit recalls of his first days, so he and Strybosch started working to clean up problems. For example, they hadn't been paying dividends on time, and only got away with this because of the loyalty the credit union engendered among members. At times, people would come in and find that a cheque they had deposited a week before still hadn't been processed. Once Strybosch and Smit got things in shape and day-to-day services became more efficient, they could concentrate on developing the business and expanding the membership.

"They [Smit and Vandenberg] changed the whole environment," Strybosch remembers. "It took a couple of months and there were no extra long coffee breaks anymore. Ans said to the ladies, 'Why would you go and drink coffee? Management doesn't do that. If you want to make good money and be someone, then act like they do.' She quietly changed the whole atmosphere. A different approach to everything."

But Strybosch wasn't limiting his vision to the London part of the operation. The administration did have to get its house in order, but Strybosch was looking at the entire credit union in Southwestern Ontario. "I felt we needed a cooperative system that would serve people better than what we had. That was the intent...to try to conquer that. Everything was geared toward that. You tried to attract people who believed that same thing. You tried to work with your Board and you carry that same feeling, that same mission and make it reality."

The credit union was hampered, somewhat, by the extent to which it could do business and compete with banks. Although the nearby and larger Niagara Credit Union was providing loans of $30,000 in the 1960s, St. Willibrord was limited to $5,000. But Strybosch recalls St. Willibrord exceeding those limits to meet members' demands and keep their business. The province would investigate when it got out of hand, but the thinking at St. Willibrord was to give more money than allowed and then watch as the province raised the limits to make it legal. By the end of December 1970, the credit union could grant farm and business loans, and could give individuals up to $10,000 without first mortgage security but were not to exceed $25,000. There is a letter in the St. Willibrord archives dated December 30, 1971 from the Department of Financial and Commercial Affairs warning the credit union to keep to its loan limits. St. Willibrord had lent money beyond the $25,000 limit. Another warning letter came in January, 1972. But Strybosch was right about how the government ultimately acted. The credit union's archives show how loan levels rose in those years. By December 1973, the limits had increased to $50,000 for individuals, while business loans couldn't exceed 15 per cent of the credit union's capital. A year later, the individual loan level jumped to $60,000.

The 1970s were also good for members. The share dividends ran in the four to five per cent range annually, going as high as 7.5 per cent in 1976. On September 17, 1974, Registered Retirement Savings Plans (RRSPs) became a service provided to members, and Registered Home Ownership Savings Plans (RHOSPs) first appeared in December, 1975. The daily interest savings account, known as Plan 24, was introduced in October, 1976. Times were good at St. Willibrord. They were benefiting from the prosperity that many Dutch Canadian immigrants were enjoying, as well as from the fact that the second generation (those immigrants' children) was starting to enter the workforce and look for a place to put their hard-earned money. Coupled with that was a banking system that still wasn't filling everyone's needs, and strong, positive word-of-mouth that St. Willibrord was getting back on track and offering more financial services.

Although Strybosch was clearly in control, he admits there were strong differences of opinion in his early years as manager. Bill Intven, long-time Board member, felt the credit union should concentrate only on London and build up the strength there. There were other differences of opinion on the Board, and Strybosch's technique was to have frequent, private discussions with Board members to make his point that St. Willibrord needed to be strong throughout Southwestern Ontario. Intven didn't always agree and would take time to write letters to Strybosch outlining some subtle advice or suggestions for a change in direction. Strybosch was impressed by Intven's feel for the credit union and often took the advice.

Other key hirings would take place throughout the 1970s as the credit union grew rapidly. A glance at today's executive reveals that several people were hired that decade: Rick Hoevenaars and Harry Joosten, to name two. It was no coincidence. Strybosch wanted young, loyal employees who were hard-working and enthusiastic to help make his vision for St. Willibrord a reality. This didn't go unnoticed at the Board level where some members were reluctant to see these young, long-haired neophytes helping to run the business. "I had so many young ones around me that they felt it had become a bit of a kindergarten," Strybosch says with a laugh. "I hired Jack and I hired Rick and I hired Harry. I was criticized. They used to say,

John Strybosch and Staff circa 1985 (Position Titles at the Time)

Front row, seated left to right: Frank Kennes (Credit Manager), Jack Smit (Assistant General Manager), John Strybosch (General Manager), Harry Wijsman (Blenheim Branch Manager), José Cozyn (Stratford Branch Manager)
Back row, standing left to right: Louis Soetemens (Arkona Branch Manager), Wally Mutsaers (London East Branch Manager), Ralph Bakker (Watford Branch Manager), Ken Peters (Strathroy Branch Manager), Rick Hoevenaars (Finance Manager), John Willemse (Sarnia Branch Manager), Jim Wincott (London Downtown Branch Manager), Harry Joosten (Member Relations Manager)

'You work with kids and all boys.' But they were flexible. You hire a kid, you can work with him. You hire one 50 years old, you never bend them anymore. That's a big difference. And they grow up. Very good people.

"That in itself is to be considered. Not only what you do directly for your members, but it is also whom you hire and how you cultivate the organization itself so that it can continue. It is very crucial, and I was totally convinced to look in their background and where they came from before I hired anyone."

It was the kind of forward-thinking that would serve St. Willibrord well in the long run.

With St. Willibrord growing at rates of 30 per cent or more per year, it appeared the future was bright. But its charter still limited membership to those who were Dutch Catholic, and their families. Some non-Dutch Catholic members came into the fold through marriage, and it's no secret that administration would look the other way when someone who didn't fit all the criteria wanted to join. Occasionally, the provincial government would rap the credit union's knuckles for it, but the practice continued. The administration at St. Willibrord knew they had to expand their bond of association if they were going to continue thriving. "The Dutch tend to integrate into the society they've moved to," explains Smit, so it was natural to want to become a *community* credit union. St. Willibrord officials had seen other religious or ethnically-based credit unions wither and die because membership regulations limited growth, and they wanted to avoid the same fate. On a few occasions in the 1960s, they had tried to convince government officials to let them admit other members outside the Catholic Church but, "It was always 'No,' whatever we asked," says Strybosch. "Whatever we did, it was always 'No.'" At one time in 1965, the credit union tried to expand its bond of association to non-Catholic Dutch and Flemish in the Diocese of London. Board members Bill Intven and John Féron argued that many non-Catholics had approached them and that they were trying to expand because the Church encouraged them to cooperate with other Christians. They received this letter from the Department of the Attorney General in August, 1965: "In my opinion, your bond of membership is already too broad. After our experience with your group, charters based on similar bonds have been refused. I understand that you have collectors ... from Sarnia to Woodstock and Seaforth. It is this unwieldy bond that is the cause of your many operational difficulties."

The message was clear in the 1960s and early 70s. Expansion wasn't an option, at least until St. Willibrord put its house in order. "To change a bond of association was almost like changing religion at that particular time," adds Féron.

As part of their increased outward-looking approach, Féron, who was Board president throughout the 1970s, got more involved with credit union organizations on a provincial and even national level, a move he felt was important to St. Willibrord's future. "We saw enormous restrictions. The restrictions of loan possibilities, business loans in particular, and farm loans. The business was getting bigger;

JOHN STRYBOSCH

John Strybosch was born on March 3, 1923, in Asten, North Brabant, the Netherlands. He was a graduate of agricultural and horticultural programs, and took courses in the social sciences, bookkeeping, general business, co-op banking services, as well as English.

In 1938, at the age of 15, he had started working on his parents' farm, becoming a member of the local Young Farmers' Organization a year later. When Germany occupied the Netherlands, this organization was officially disbanded, but members continued to meet in an unofficial capacity to develop sports and recreational programs. At the end of the War, he was elected to the local Board of the YFO and then went on to serve on the District Board. In 1948 he became chairman of the District Board of the Young Farmers. That same year, he was elected to the Board of his local Boerenleenbank (Farmers' Lending Bank) cooperative, where he subsequently served as chairman from 1949 until 1951.

In 1951, after carefully weighing all his options, Strybosch decided that the best opportunities for his family lay in Canada. One of his uncles had previously emigrated in 1928, settling in Watford. Another had come to Canada in 1950 with his 12 children and they seemed to be doing fine. John Strybosch had been head of his family since his parents died in 1946 and 1947. The family farm was sold, and on July 10, 1951, he became a landed immigrant in Canada, settling near Strathroy, Ontario. At first, he took on a number of different jobs including work in a restaurant, and then in the Strathroy Glass Factory.

Through the Dutch Catholic community, Strybosch learned of the efforts by Father Jan van Wezel to establish a credit union in the area. He was to become member number 28 and served on the early Board of Directors. It became his responsibility as a fieldman to gather money and deal with members in the outlying areas. He also assisted local collectors in Strathroy, Parkhill, Grand Bend, and Watford. Part of his responsibility was to track down delinquent loans and promote the credit union concept to non-members.

In 1953, John returned to the Netherlands to marry Helena (Lena) Maria Aarts whom he had known before coming to Canada. In 1958, he started a bookkeeping business which grew to serve 400 clients and employed 4 people. During this time, Strybosch served as cashier for the Strathroy district and was elected to the Strathroy advisory committee. In 1964, John and Lena moved to Arkona and helped establish a branch office of the credit union there. They lived in the back quarters of the same building. As secretary-cashier for the Arkona Division, Strybosch was responsible for Thedford, Grand Bend, Strathroy, Watford, Wyoming, Forest, and Parkhill.

On November 7, 1968, John Strybosch was again elected to the Board of Directors of the credit union. However, when the general manager resigned his position, John was asked to take over. From February, 1969 until his retirement on March 31, 1988, Strybosch served as general manager and oversaw the restructuring and regeneration of what is now St. Willibrord Community Credit Union.

Through his ongoing efforts and dedication to the credit union concept, John Strybosch earned the respect and loyalty of staff and members by setting clear policies and establishing long-term, achievable goals for the organization.

Lena and John Strybosch before leaving the Netherlands

it was not small groups of people anymore. [We wanted] a wider scope. We felt that was the way to go. As such, in the first ten or fifteen years of our existence, we had worked mainly on the solid building of our membership and making sure they were good members. We got that, now let's expand this a bit further and start using all the opportunities around us.

"I saw that if we were going to fulfill that potential, we had to be bigger. Here in London, for instance, we had 55 or 60 credit unions, all small. We saw the credit union, not just as a small financial institution. It had to be, for us, *the* financial institution, just as we were used to having in Europe with the Farmers' Bank. So, we had very much the idea that we had to expand. One of the ways was by getting a person like myself onto the Provincial Board. I believe I was one of the first two immigrants elected to that particular Board."

Officials at St. Willibrord had watched other larger credit unions grow, particularly VanCity Savings in Vancouver and Niagara Credit Union which served a similar kind of clientele. If those credit unions could grow and prosper, why couldn't St. Willibrord? "As in any business, it was just the moment you have to dare to throw things open and carry the consequences," said Féron. "So that we did."

The timing was right. Although portions of the new Credit Unions Act of 1976 weren't officially proclaimed until about six years later, it did allow for credit unions with full-time management and sufficient capital to operate under open bonds, free of the usual restrictions of membership. By the time St. Willibrord celebrated its 25th Anniversary in 1976, it was a fast-growing and prosperous credit union with 6,000 members and more than $15 million in assets. At the same time it was enjoying this prosperity, another large credit union in London was experiencing tough times. Co-op Services (London) Credit Union had been operating a few years longer than St. Willibrord, but it had around 5,000 members in the early 70s and about $4 million in assets. Nick Van Osch had joined the Board of Co-op Services in 1972, and he recalled it had a history of bad management. "Their office was on the corner of King and Talbot Streets, in the little corner store there. It was really dingy and bad. They had been talking for years about building

Nick Van Osch
Board Chair
1986-98

a nice office, you know, and putting this credit union on the map. These decisions had all been made just about when I got there. They had bought the land at 131 Wharncliffe Road, and hired an architect to design the building. That building, built in 1973, turned out to be too expensive and probably in the wrong location. It was a $500,000 building and with assets of four and a half million, that would eat up more than 10 per cent of the assets. The norm is about three per cent. These things I didn't know anything about, of course, being new at this. Of course, that drove that credit union deeper in the hole. Losses were staggering."

In 1974, a dispute between Co-op Services Board president Fred Gale, and the manager Dave Harding, led to Harding's termination and the hiring of Bill Chalmers, formerly a branch manager from the Bank of Montreal in Thorold, near St. Catharines. Despite hiring a new manager, the situation didn't improve. "You see, a credit union manager and a bank manager are two different animals," Van Osch explained. "A credit union manager has to be a general manager. A Bank of Montreal manager is a branch manager. They have all the policies, all the rules and regulations in place. You do this and that and that, then everything will be just fine. He wasn't used to dealing with a Board. Things were never smooth. Then we hired an accountant to try to get things under control. Things went from bad to worse. They never improved."

That situation led to other Board members stepping down, and Van Osch had to scramble to get new directors to help him out. In 1974, he was elected president, and because he knew people at St. Willibrord, he started considering a closer relationship with them. "[Our Board] said, 'Take it from here. It seems like you're the most experienced person here.' Which I wasn't and I was. Just not enough experience, but at least I had some," Van Osch recalled. "So we carried on from there. Then I took up contact with John Strybosch. I finally said that this was it. I've got new directors now and the old ones are gone so I'm going to be a bit more cozy with St. Willibrord. Because they were never close, these two credit unions, you see. So I contacted John. I said, 'Look, I've got all these problems and I don't know what to do. We need help.' I [asked him if he would] come to our Board meetings and guide us through things that we should be doing right. He did. He came down and listened a lot, never said anything and he took a lot of notes. Then he would say, 'Well you should do this. You should do that.'"

According to Van Osch, Co-op Services wasn't well regarded by other small credit unions in London because it was drawing members from them. It was seen as "the big bad guy in town," except, apparently, by St. Willibrord. "At St. Willibrord, they weren't too afraid of us. It was that funny Dutch credit union that was out there somewhere and didn't bother anybody. But John Strybosch wanted something different for St. Willibrord." In 1975, Van Osch and Strybosch started talking.

Both agreed that Co-op Services wasn't going to solve its problems on its own and was stuck with a white elephant of a building on Wharncliffe Road. Strybosch knew this was the opportunity St. Willibrord had been waiting for, a chance in one move to get the community Bond of Association. There were mixed feelings about it on the St. Willibrord Board but, "Gradually, step by step, we came to the conclusion that it would be the best move," he says. As part of the planning process for such a merger, Intven drafted a 39-point paper that raised questions that needed to be answered before any such move could take place. It's the kind of strategic approach more commonplace today, but in 1975, this was an exceptionally wise and cautious move. If St. Willibrord were going to become a community credit union, it would have to be on its own terms and to the benefit of all members. St. Willibrord offered a more extensive product line than Co-op Services and, "We knew from the high demand of lending in the agricultural sector that we had to have a stronghold in the city," adds Smit. In fact, the negotiations that took place between the two credit unions set a new model for how mergers would take place. Things like analysing loans of another credit union and its assets hadn't been done before. "In the past, a credit union might look at the book deficit, but we looked at the loans and the buildings. We looked at it as a business," says Smit.

Strybosch particularly recalls the first meeting of Board members from both sides in early March, 1976. The night before, Strybosch and Smit had gone to the Latin Quarter restaurant on Maple Street (now Dufferin Avenue) and, over several Harvey Wallbangers, discussed the credit union's future. Despite hangovers the next day and Strybosch's promise to himself that he wouldn't drink again "for a while", the next meeting with Co-op Services took place again at the Latin Quarter. One Co-op Services member insisted Strybosch have a drink and, "I could not say 'No' to a friendly man," Strybosch says with a smile. A vicious ice storm that night kept everyone inside for hours, and Strybosch laughs now about how the alcohol may have smoothed relations between the two Boards' members that night.

The St. Willibrord administration had some reservations about Co-op Services because of its financial difficulties and different makeup of members. A St. Willibrord member tended to be more of an entrepreneurial, small business operator while Co-op's were more blue-collar wage earners. Some wondered if there might be a clash of cultures.

Nevertheless, Smit remembers that first meeting at the Latin Quarter as "very positive, right from the start." Fortunately for St. Willibrord, Van Osch was an early ally in this merger. He knew that Co-op Services needed help, that the provincial government was concerned about his credit union's deficits, and that the new headquarters was a financial drain. He recalls that it took some selling to convince his members the merger was wise, but with the problems they faced, it made sense. Meanwhile at St. Willibrord, there was opposition, but it was slight. St. Willibrord simply wanted to make sure that, if the merger took place, it would be done to its satisfaction.

A letter dated November 2, 1976, from Intven to the Ontario Credit Union League, says a merger would be conditional on getting a full community charter for the total geographic area that St. Willibrord had. OCUL replied about two weeks later suggesting St. Willibrord apply for "open bond" under Section 27 (2) of the new Credit Unions Act. This would allow them to accept new members regardless of residence.

It would, however, be several years before St. Willibrord got that wish. At the time it was talking with Co-op Services, it was also looking to take over the Forest Community Credit Union. Moore Credit Union, based in Sarnia, opposed the deal because it felt it had more jurisdiction in that part of Lambton County and had also started with an ethnic Dutch base. Even though the Forest members preferred to join with St. Willibrord, the government ruled that it fell within Moore's jurisdiction. As well, nearby Sydenham Credit Union, in Strathroy, did not want to see St. Willibrord have an open bond in west Middlesex and east Lambton counties.

A merger of this size had never taken place among credit unions in Ontario. In many respects, both sides and the government were entering virgin territory. In 1977, the government was also putting in place the Ontario Shares and Deposits Insurance Corporation (OSDIC). The Stabilization Fund set up by OCUL to protect credit union members' savings had been starting to make payouts to cover deficits for the past few years. The negotiators from St. Willibrord were adamant about one condition: they would not take financial responsibility for the building on Wharncliffe Road. They were also unwilling to pay dividends that year to former Co-op Services members once the merger took place. At one point, these obstacles made it look as if the merger might not happen. They were prepared to walk away if the conditions weren't right. On the plus side, however, St. Willibrord members, particularly rural ones who saw a merger leading to an influx of deposits available to them for loans, favoured the marriage of the two credit unions. The government was hesitant about the merger at first, but eventually agreed to take over the building and lease it back to St. Willibrord. In May 1977, a letter from F.C. Croswell of the Stabilization Fund guaranteed that the Fund would stabilize the operation of Co-op Services at the time of the merger so "there will be no loss to the members." And finally, the Ministry of Consumer and Commercial Relations wrote a letter on July 8, 1977 to confirm that agreement in principle had been reached regarding St. Willibrord going from an association to a community-type credit union. But only for the city of London.

Another stumbling block was the name. It wouldn't be the first or last time St. Willibrord Community Credit Union considered a name change. While St. Willibrord was the larger of the two, with $17 million in assets compared to $4.5 million, some Co-op Services people wanted a name change away from St. Willibrord when the merger took place. Those who wanted a change found St. Willibrord unwieldy to say, and believed it didn't fully reflect the makeup of the proposed community organization. As early as 1976, some people on both sides were considering the name "WillCo Credit Union" to reflect the merger.

"Some thought [the merger talk] was a promise to change the name and others thought it was a promise to look at it," remembers Harry Joosten, who was a relatively new employee then. "There was a real controversy there. People picked the name issue as their standard bearer for how they were feeling. [They thought] if you changed the name, you're no longer the Dutch Catholic credit union." But by then, through marriage and business relationships, 10 to 15 per cent of members were not Dutch Catholics anyway. Regardless of how the name issue was to be solved, everything else needed to allow a merger to occur was in place by July 1977; it was now up to both sides to determine whether to begin a new phase in credit union history.

A meeting was set up on the lower floor of Centennial Hall in London on July 20, 1977, for St. Willibrord members to vote. Joosten recalls the atmosphere among members at the time. "People felt they had to do this to grow and increase their services. If we take them over we grow, we get a community bond, and we prevent substantial negative public reaction to [Co-op Services] potential failure." A two-thirds majority was needed for the takeover motion to pass; when the votes were tallied, it was close to unanimous. A cheer went up when it was announced that St. Willibrord members had favoured a merger. Meanwhile, members of Co-op Services were meeting in the lobby of their building on Wharncliffe Road. "Our vote was already completed and we were still waiting to hear," he says. "We kept calling, and finally a half dozen of their members came to Centennial Hall to celebrate. The merger had been accepted by them, too."

In retrospect, the question could be asked: Would St. Willibrord be around today if the merger hadn't taken place, Co-op Services hadn't survived, and a community bond of association had been refused? With more than 20 years of hindsight, Jack Smit isn't so sure. "I don't know that we'd have gained a community charter if we hadn't merged." But John Féron believes the strengths that had made St. Willibrord thrive into the 1970s would have overcome those obstacles. "We would have found other ways," he says firmly. "Co-op Services was certainly not our salvation. Co-op Services was in dire need to join us. The only thing they had to offer to us was their bond of association. Certainly, nothing else. It was a means to an end, a means of getting to where we wanted to go."

The official merger took place on October 1, 1977, the first day of St. Willibrord's fiscal year and, coincidentally, the same date that OSDIC was incorporated. St. Willibrord had agreed to take on all the Co-op Services members who wanted to join as well as the staff. It leased the Wharncliffe Road building for three years from OSDIC, which assumed ownership of the property, and the Stabilization Fund provided an extra reserve for the expected increase in loans. The merger also meant that St. Willibrord would be offering Saturday hours to its members; Joosten recalls going over to Wharncliffe Road on October 1st with Féron and Strybosch to greet their newest members coming through the door. Although it only extended to the city of London's borders at this point, St. Willibrord finally had its community bond.

Business continued to hum throughout the late 1970s. There were, of course, adjustments to be made now that they'd had an influx of Co-op Services members. The Board had added two seats to recognize this change in make-up, with Nick Van Osch and Paul Kiteley, formerly of Co-op Services, taking their place at the

Opening day Wharncliffe Road branch, October 1, 1977
John Féron, Nick Van Osch, and John Strybosch greeting a member

St. Willibrord table with the other directors. St. Willibrord also expanded its London branch advisory committee from three to five members, adding two former Co-op directors to it. The annual meeting the following year had something of an adversarial tone with new members asking more questions than was the norm at these gatherings, but eventually they returned to the more consensus-building approach favoured by long-time St. Willibrord members.

Despite getting its community bond in London, St. Willibrord executives were still eager to expand that type of association to other counties in Southwestern Ontario. In other branches, outside London, membership was still to be limited to Dutch and Flemish Catholics. The provincial government felt that London was a wide enough bond for the moment and that discussions with other credit unions in Strathroy, Parkhill and elsewhere needed to be conducted first. Because of the recent merger, London was the only large city in Ontario to be served by a single community credit union. Féron said at the time, "The merger will help us to promote the credit union idea, not just St. Willibrord. We want people to join a credit union. They have a wide choice, some fifty, in the London area."

The credit union's approach to its bond of association was based on the honour system. Potential members who filled out the application form, simply signed a statement saying they had read the rules concerning bond of association and declared themselves eligible.

St. Willibrord did attract some government attention because of advertisements it ran in *The London Free Press* seeking new members. The ads did not specifically point out the limitations of the bond of association and, because the *Free Press* had subscribers in many counties around London, the ads were seen not only by people in London, to whom they were directed, but also by readers throughout much of Southwestern Ontario. A couple of other credit unions believed St. Willibrord was overstepping its London boundaries. St. Willibrord argued they were competing more with banks and trust companies in the area than credit unions and could also offer a wider range of services to people. One credit union launched a formal complaint about it with the provincial government, but it only led to St. Willibrord being gently admonished. Nothing more serious took place.

Meanwhile, St. Willibrord remained open to approaches from other smaller credit unions and, during the late 70s and early 80s, absorbed a number of smaller units in Southwestern Ontario through purchase and sale agreements. Some had run into trouble because of too much capital spending, while others simply wanted to become part of a larger organization with access to its many services. By January 1981, bylaws had been passed which expanded the charter to include the entire counties of Lambton and Middlesex, the city of Stratford, and the town of Blenheim. Elgin County was added in 1989. Starting with Co-op Services Credit Union, other credit unions which have amalgamated with St. Willibrord include Blenheim Community Credit Union, St. Joseph's Parish in Sarnia, and Northern Telecom Credit Union in London in 1992. The company had closed its local plant and about 2,000 former employees transferred their memberships. With this expansion, St. Willibrord was becoming a community credit union for virtually all of Southwestern Ontario.

Building new branch offices, and benefiting from a fairly buoyant economy, St. Willibrord continued to grow and expand. But the good times wouldn't last. The dividend rate paid on shares to members dropped to 2.75 per cent in 1979, which was the lowest since 1957. The situation would get worse over the next two years when rates dropped to zero. By 1981, the economy slowed, interest rates skyrocketed, and St. Willibrord hit a wall that would remain in place for many months. According to Van Osch, there were a few Board members who grumbled that the takeover of Co-op Services was one reason why St. Willibrord started facing financial difficulties. "There was still much animosity, you know, like at Board meetings. We had caucus meetings where I used to take a lot of flack. Finally, I said to John [Strybosch], 'Look, I'm fed up with this crap. You deal with them.' Because even the president of the credit union at the time, John Féron, quite often kind of hinted that maybe we made a mistake. I said, 'What's done is done, and you benefited.' It's simple. Dutch immigration is not growing. Those who are here have become Canadian. My grandchildren, like all my kids, are members of the credit union. But how many families do you have like that? Eventually, this dies off. Kids move away. There was a base, but the base wasn't growing any more. So, John Strybosch had this right. He said that we must become a *community* credit union."

While there were some financial burdens that accompanied the takeover, the real problem from 1979 to about 1982 was that the credit union had a mismatch of loans because of soaring interest rates. "Right after we had done all this expansion, the economy came to a grinding halt, interest rates shot up, and asset/liability management was something we learned about after," Smit recalls. The credit union's loan demand was so strong that it was borrowing to keep pace. The trouble was that members were given loans at fixed rates but the credit union was borrowing at variable rates which were increasing and that caused a gap. "It was a tough time," Smit says, in something of an understatement. Despite the gloom, Smit and others today say they were never at the point where they thought they'd fold. Says Strybosch: "Most mortgages with us at that time were for a three year term, and we knew that we would get a chance to make up the difference."

The Board considered stopping loans altogether, but there was tremendous resistance to that. What the credit union did as soon as it figured out its troubles was first to limit mortgages to $50,000, and then impose a full moratorium. This period in the early 80s was the first time in its history that St. Willibrord suffered significant losses. "I think panic might be an exaggeration," Smit says now, "but it was certainly a time of great anxiety." Essentially, the executives felt that all they needed was time, time from the members to let them handle the problem and time for a change in interest rates to kick in.

At its darkest hour, around February, 1981, St. Willibrord was losing as much as $2,000 a day. "There were nights when I know John was not sleeping well." Projections were made based on how loans were being paid up and how money was coming in, essentially how long it would take to see light at the end of this very dark tunnel. Estimates were only about one month out. "But in that time, we lost a lot of money." The Board accepted Smit's projections and "the members were not disturbed. They had total trust in us. The Board was anxious too, but they had trust and confidence in us, and we did turn the corner. Our members were pretty loyal because we'd had five or six years of strong growth up to then. We had built up a level of confidence."

But if Ontario Shares and Deposits Insurance Corporation lost patience, it could ask the credit union to close its doors. In fact, Smit recalls a visit by the CEO of OSDIC. "He looked at me and said, 'You've lost a lot of weight' and I said, 'Well these are lean years.'" He laughs now at the memory, but Smit says that at one point OSDIC, in 1982, did make an approach to take over supervision of the credit union. The St. Willibrord management and Board resisted, knowing it would lead to their losing control. This had been their credit union for 30 years; they had fought adversity before and had succeeded. "We said, 'No'" Smit says. "By that time, we already knew we were on the path to recovery and felt we could do it better on our own."

One factor that might have helped them was that most other credit unions were in the same situation. In May 1982, the OSDIC sent a letter saying that "loans receivable have decreased so member credit unions should persevere with a policy of granting loans only if deposits are available to match the required terms and after the credit risk has been thoroughly evaluated." Essentially, the government kept its hands off, but such a scenario might not play out that way today. Canadians, at the time, perceived financial institutions as being strong and able to weather most storms. Few would have considered that such organizations could go bankrupt. But since then, trust companies and other institutions have folded. Today, there would be more scrutiny from members and the media if a credit union were to go through such a long period of losses.

In the end, St. Willibrord experienced 23 months of losses, worth about $1.3 million. It would take more than four years before they made back the money they lost. What Smit and others learned was to keep a better handle on asset/liability management and to turn their back on the heady days of 30 per cent plus growth. From now on, targeted growth would be no more than 10 to 15 per cent per year. Like any crisis survived, it made St. Willibrord stronger, better, and able to cope with the future.

With that kind of experience under his belt, Jack Smit could confidently take over management of the credit union when John Strybosch decided to retire in 1988. The age of "J.S. Superstar," as an employee-performed musical tribute to Strybosch called him, was over. St. Willibrord had come through the fiercest of financial storms and was now poised to face the challenges of its fifth decade.

MEMORIES

José Cozyn, who acted as branch manager of the Stratford Branch from 1969 to 1994, remembers how John Strybosch came to inspect the construction site of their new branch office in 1974. "He stepped on a board and fell through the floor joist and got stuck. Bill and I helped him up because he'd had his hands in his pockets. We asked if he was hurt but he said, "No!" Half an hour later, John was as white as a ghost. We quickly took him home then looked at his leg. What a mess! He limped for weeks."

Peter De Bruyn remembers how John, back in the late 1950s, was fieldman for St. Willibrord. "He would drive around in his Volkswagen, visiting members with all kinds of problems, and try to solve them. I'm sure that was not an easy task but he did it very well."

John and Lena with Volkswagen

"After I applied for financing at the credit union for my farm," recalls Ted Donkers, "John came out to the farm for a look.

"Following a tour of the barns and yard he said, 'You know, you're asking for a lot of money.'

"That got me worried, but we did get the loan. Afterwards, John met me and said,'Do you know what I told the Credit Committee? I told them it was a mess outside, but the pigs looked excellent, which I didn't expect.'

"That's John for you. He always had a soft spot for the farmers and knew when he saw a good one."

At his gala retirement party in 1988, the staff of St. Willibrord put on a humorous, musical skit called "J.S. Superstar". With a nod to the hit musical *Jesus Christ Superstar,* lyrics to some songs were creatively re-written to reflect and remember the high points in his career. The performance, by Central Office staff, delighted John and Lena Strybosch and all members of the large audience.

AT THE TIME

St. Willibrord officials, who were anxiously waiting for the news on whether Co-op Services would join forces with them, weren't the only ones sweating it out on July 20, 1977.

Anyone living in London and Southwestern Ontario that day was experiencing the longest heat wave the area had seen in 31 years. A temperature of 36 degrees Celsius, with a humidex reading of 41 degrees, was forecast and in those days people were still unfamiliar enough with the new metric way of measuring that the London Free Press also provided information in Fahrenheit: 97 and 105 degrees respectively.

Several people had already died in the U.S. because of the hot weather, and Londoners were buying air conditioners and fans at triple the normal rate. Whether it was the heat or not, a Reverend Leslie of Mississauga was in the news that day for changing his mind about performing a nude wedding that week at the Miss Nude World Pageant. He had earlier told reporters he was going to do the ceremony for his usual $75 fee, but changed his mind because it might harm his reputation as a minister.

In the House of Commons in Ottawa, things were heating up over a bill that was passed designed to deny cheaters and loafers unemployment insurance benefits. The bill called for an increase in the time a person must work to get the benefits and reduced the amount of time anyone could receive the benefits. Manpower Minister Bud Cullen said at least 50,000 people could be removed from the unemployment insurance rolls by this legislation.

Politicians were also buzzing about the CRTC endorsing a report that said the CBC was not living up to its mandate of developing national unity. In fact, several Liberals in Pierre Trudeau's government felt that Radio-Canada was riddled with pro-separatists. Pierre wasn't the only Trudeau in the headlines that day. His estranged wife, Margaret, was keeping reporters and photographers hopping because she was in New York to catch a performance of *Swan Lake* by the National Ballet of Canada.

The media were being blamed by former PM John Diefenbaker for being far too critical of the still relatively new Conservative Leader, Joe Clark. Diefenbaker also thought that recent gun legislation passed by the Liberals was a gross tragedy.

A tragedy of a different sort in B.C.

was also grabbing attention as police continued to look for a killer who fatally shot two teenagers and may have killed two others in the Fraser Valley. And folks in Rosa, Manitoba, were recovering from a tornado that had ripped through their town causing about $500,000 damage and killing two people.

Internationally, Israeli PM Menachem Begin and U.S. President Jimmy Carter were meeting in Washington to try and make progress in Mideast peace talks. Begin did not want to withdraw from the occupied West Bank of Jordan. And a report from Washington said that aerosol sprays may be doing more damage to the earth's ozone layer than previously thought.

Back at home, Mingles ran an ad boasting itself as London's longest and friendliest dance floor, while the Firehall played up its country/bluegrass performers and Fryfogles was serving up the blues. The New Yorker cinema was showing *A Star is Born* and other top movies at the time were *New York, New York* at the Arcade 2, *Smokey and the Bandit* at the Odeon 1, and *Star Wars* at the Twilite Drive In. The "hot" movie arriving in a few days at the Capitol was *The Island of Dr. Moreau* starring Burt Lancaster and Michael York.

In sports, the National League All-Star team defeated their American League counterparts 7 to 5 the previous night in New York, notching their 14th victory over the American League in 15 games. Going into the game, the Blue Jays and the Atlanta Braves had the worst records in baseball that season.

Anyone grocery shopping that week could go to Meatland and buy steaks at $1.49 a pound and ground beef at 85 cents a pound. Loblaws advertised four heads of lettuce for one dollar, a one-pound package of wieners cost 59 cents, a package of Gillette razor blades was $1.54, and chicken legs or breasts were $1 a pound. Over at the A & P, Tide was $1.99 for a five pound box, large eggs were 77 cents a dozen, and three loaves of white bread cost a dollar.

Highbury Ford was advertising a 1976 Pinto wagon with 16,000 miles for $2,988 while Central Chev Olds had a 1977 half ton van for $4,864. Unfurnished apartments were in the $200 to $250 a month range for one and two bedrooms, while a three-bedroom bungalow in Byron was selling for $54,900 and a two-storey, four bedroom house in Westmount was advertised at $72,900.

St. Willibrord members might not have appreciated it at the time, but on July 20, 1977, the U.S. dollar was worth $1.06 Canadian.

Roots &
Branches

Growth and Evolution

CHAPTER 5

When John Strybosch retired in 1988 and Jack Smit took over, the credit union had come through some tough years triumphantly. Members and staff had stuck together, weathered the storm of high interest rates and mismatched loans, and were now on the brink of a new era for St. Willibrord. To outsiders, it might have seemed strange that so few members had been upset by those troubled times, but it was the overall make-up of the credit union and its strong agricultural and entrepreneurial roots that brought it into the late 80s intact. A lot of members having businesses of their own knew what it was like, especially farmers who knew you couldn't usually have seven good years in a row. They were going to stay with the credit union that had served them well through their own difficult years.

That feeling of sticking together through good and bad times is ultimately what makes the credit union strong. Harry Joosten notes, "It's a matter of a long-term view, and open communication that go along with trust and loyalty, and it's a matter of integrating things so that they fit together and need each other. It also relates to good, personal service and individual relationships. If you have all those things ticking, that can be a very powerful thing."

A quick look at the years 1989-91 show how stable and strong the credit union had become. In 1989, it was the 31st largest credit union in Canada and seventh largest in Ontario. By 1991, it was 28th and sixth respectively. It would continue to improve on those numbers until the end of the decade when it was 21st and fifth respectively. It can be argued that the successes of the 1990s are a direct result of the problems that took place in the early 1980s. The credit union emerged stronger and ready to move forward toward its goal of being the preferred financial institution of Southwestern Ontario. In fact, the 1988 annual report provided newly-worded objectives to reflect what the credit union was already doing and where it was heading.

The Objectives were:

To provide quality services at favourable terms.

To build lasting relationships with our members through respect for their dignity and self-worth.

To be directed by representatives elected by active, informed members.

To attract capable people and provide a stimulating environment in which they can work and build a career.

To be efficient, manage risk and generate profit to build a strong capital base.

To be a good neighbour in our local communities.

To be active participants in the cooperative system.

To maintain good relations with all levels of government on a non-partisan basis.

To show that cooperation works well.

For the credit union to meet or keep meeting these objectives, changes would have to be made, and certainly Smit was now going to put his stamp on the credit union's development. He was no longer Strybosch's right-hand man; he was in charge.

Smit had been groomed for the job for several years, but knew he still had to establish himself with a staff that was used to the Strybosch style. "I had good credibility," Smit says. "I know they knew me as a finance person interested in dollars and cents and profit and all that. John was the 'people guy'. That's how the staff perceived it, so I did a number of things, like instituting staff surveys to get feedback. Then I shared results and reported what I was going to do to make things even better. I did a number of things that were not profit-driven. So I think I established myself in the new position fairly quickly."

The Smit years have been times of great change for the credit union as technology and increased competition among financial institutions have become more prevalent. Change was nothing new at St. Willibrord. Its entire history was one of anticipating change, adapting to particular circumstances, and coming up with solutions to keep members satisfied. It had always been a forward-looking credit union that lobbied hard to become a full-service institution. When members had wanted chequing accounts in the 1950s, St. Willibrord went against the grain of standard credit union practice and offered them. Rick Hoevenaars, Vice-President Finance, says another key innovation the credit union first introduced in Ontario was weekly mortgage payments to allow people to reduce their amortization period and pay off their houses more quickly. That came about after senior credit union officials saw a story about how a Caisse Populaire in Quebec was offering weekly mortgage payments. They decided such a system was a good fit for them and members and introduced the concept in the early 1980s. Although banks at the time pooh-poohed the idea, the concept garnered much media attention and proved popular with members. "It took off and now it's a way of life."

But that's almost always been the St. Willibrord way. When members wanted higher loan levels, longer hours, a range of savings plans, and automatic banking, the credit union either led the way or responded quickly. They wanted to anticipate change, meet it, or hear what members wanted, and respond to it. It was a philosophy that had served the credit union well for its first 40 years. The 1990s would be no different.

For much of its history, St. Willibrord had moved ahead by offering different products to members. In the 90s, they were introducing new products such as the Fat Cat® and HeadStart® accounts for young owners, the Prima® Mortgage that offered flexible payments, and the Connexion™ chequing package that provided rewards for doing more business with the credit union. But as members became more sophisticated in their understanding of financial matters and increasingly demanding of what their credit union could offer, having a range of products became almost a given. The St. Willibrord administration was also becoming more sophisticated and believed it had to create a different environment for its members, one that would be described now as "relationship banking".

Smit knew St. Willibrord had always had a strong service culture, but "not what I would call a sales culture. Then I set out to deliberately change that. There was a lot of resistance. 'No, no, we're doing member service,' they'd say. Well, you know member service is to establish what needs they have for a product although they may not be familiar with the product or realize that it would be a good product for them. And that is really sales." Smit had read about other financial institutions focusing more on measuring sales and overall performance.

WHAT'S IN A NAME?

"Owner" versus "member" … versus customer, client, borrower, annuitant, shareholder, voter … the list goes on. Just what do we call the people who have joined St. Willibrord and chosen it to fulfil their financial service needs?

Up until the mid to late 1990s, the predominant term at St. Willibrord and within the credit union system was "member". At the time, it was a point of differentiation: banks and trust companies had customers, but credit unions served their members. "Customer" was not acceptable; its use was forbidden to staff even though many people referred to themselves as such.

More recently, however, other financial service providers, most notably American Express, started using the "m-word" more prominently. As well, research conducted by St. Willibrord indicated that "membership" was still confusing to a large part of the public, even potentially a barrier to beginning a relationship with the credit union. Some people were making mental links to trade union membership or to exclusive club membership.

By looking again at just what set credit unions in general, and St. Willibrord in particular, apart from the rest of the industry, it became evident that people most likely to deal with St. Willibrord were those who valued ownership. They owned not just their financial institution but also they owned their future by being both responsible for, and in control of, it.

Gradually, "owner" came to replace "member" in the credit union's lexicon, especially in 1998 when St. Willibrord made a concerted internal effort to complete the transition.

In the remainder of this book, you will see both terms used. "Member" sometimes appears when the person telling the story or being quoted has used that word. "Owner" shows up more and more often toward the end. Unlike the Montagues and the Capulets, however, owners and members get along famously.

Tania Goodine was hired in 1990 to help realize that shift. As sales and marketing manager, she knew the credit union had to look beyond the everyday service they had always provided if it were to grow. Branches had always been friendly, open places that would give members what they asked for, but providing advice and informing people on what other financial products they could also consider became important. "Over the past 10 years, the whole culture has become more proactive," Goodine says about the shift in attitudes. "We still want to give you what you need, but we want to talk to you and understand what you need. A more conscious effort is made to demonstrate the benefits of doing the majority of your business with St. Willibrord and how we can offer better, more relevant advice based on that understanding."

Even 10 years ago, a member who went into the credit union asking for a chequing account would get that and very little else. Now, thanks to a range of training programs for staff, members can expect a more integrated approach to handling money, she says. "So you walk out feeling you've been taken care of. A real sense of confidence is instilled."

That doesn't mean St. Willibrord staff became pushy salespeople in the 90s, but they did begin building deeper relationships with owners to ensure that their total banking needs were taken care of. It has meant that staff throughout St. Willibrord have taken on more of an advice-giving role. One might argue that the personal nature of doing business at St. Willibrord over the years has always been central to their philosophy, and Goodine doesn't disagree. But now there are formal mechanisms in place to ensure that it's part of the credit union's daily culture. In the old days, there were people who handled deposits and others who handled loans. There was little, if any, crossover and members who wanted both types of service would shuffle from one office to the other to get their needs met. "That wasn't efficient," adds Smit. "But that was the way it was always done. For another product we sent them elsewhere, and it didn't make sense."

When owners visit a branch, they'll find at least one financial adviser on staff. They'll sit down for a longer visit and discuss their financial needs related to accounts, credit, RRSPs, mutual funds, and automatic banking. In some cases, St. Willibrord is not providing all these products directly but is outsourcing them to other providers. "What St. Willibrord brings to the table is the advice and expertise to help them choose exactly what they need," Goodine explains.

She describes the new culture as "proactive, not pushy." Annual member surveys had rated the credit union extremely high for efficiency and friendliness, but proactivity had always been slightly lower. The latter fact was established by some questions related to the degree to which staff reminded members of upcoming renewal dates for investments, loans, or mortgages, and the frequency with which staff informed members of new products, services, and other changes. By the late 90s, though, that was improving. In fact, other credit unions across Canada have met with St. Willibrord officials to find out their secret in making this shift. Goodine smiles when she recalls how some credit unions have asked to buy the St. Willibrord manual on how to do relationship banking. "There is no manual. It's just our way of doing business."

In 1997, the credit union introduced telephone banking, which has both automated and call centre links. It's proven to be a popular option. In the first year, there were 13,000 automated calls per month and about 1,000 handled by the call centre. The following year, the numbers had grown to 17,000 and 2,500 calls respectively. By March 2000, these had grown to 21,500 and 5,500. PC banking was introduced in April 1999, and Goodine doesn't rule out the possibility that the opportunity to buy stocks and bonds from St. Willibrord will also happen. She describes the credit union's approach to all these new trends as "an agile follower" that makes sure members continue to be served well by the products and available technology.

All these changes have not led to a change in the credit union's belief in face-to-face service, however. While the need for tellers may decrease as the need for financial advisers grows, St. Willibrord still continues with the smiling faces and the friendly atmosphere. "The dynamics of in-branch visits are changing," Goodine says. "We'll see members less often, but we'll see them for a financial planning chat rather than their coming in to get $100."

There weren't only innovations in the way business was done at St. Willibrord. By the 90s, the way the buildings actually looked changed too. Certainly, one of the biggest changes in the decade was the move from the Albert Street headquarters in 1993 to the new offices on Central Avenue. Goodine remembers the Albert Street office as being "outdated, too cramped and old to handle the new realities". So the new Central Avenue headquarters were designed and built to accommodate what was a new, developing culture.

St. Willibrord hired First Financial Building Corporation of St. Louis, Missouri, to help them with the design. The company had already introduced new designs to banks and credit unions in North

America, and St. Willibrord felt it was time to have this look themselves. Anyone who recalls what the old building looked like, or remembers how branches were set up, will know that the new look is clearly different. Today's credit union has more private offices where staff can fully discuss finances, and fewer teller wickets to handle the day-to-day transactions. That doesn't mean line-ups are longer, though, because other innovations such as automated and telephone banking have meant less teller business and reduced the need for wickets. Although issues of design may seem insignificant to the overall financial picture, Goodine says the buildings are often the first impression a new member will get. "They're more professional-looking so that builds confidence when a person walks through the door. Here's a stable, up-to-date modern place where I can feel safe putting my money."

"The new office design helps make it easier to handle the more complex business members are increasingly bringing to the credit union," adds Hoevenaars. That's why you'll find someone at the front reception desk of Central Avenue who can help direct you to the place you want to go. "It puts a more friendly face to it, and people aren't lost coming into the branch as to who to talk to or where to go." For the administrative staff, who share the Central Avenue building with the London Downtown branch, offices offer privacy, often a window view, and more space to meet with clients. In late 1998, a section of the basement that had been empty, except for some shelves and old equipment, was renovated to house the credit union's data centre.

Once the Central Avenue office was completed, St. Willibrord started updating the look at all its branches to better reflect the way it does business. And, in fact, more recent re-designs will devote even less space to tellers than what's available on Central Avenue. When people walk in, they'll find a large, comfortable waiting area, a children's play area and, most notably, several offices where staff can handle the owners' business. It's a warm, inviting look that doesn't scream "sell, sell, sell", but does have literature about what St. Willibrord can offer subtly displayed at key points. Instead of stacks of paper and filing cabinets filling the offices, people are more likely to see a computer on every desk and even a sitting area where they can meet with a financial adviser side-by-side to discuss their money rather than having to peer across a desk waiting to hear words of wisdom. This new look has been carefully thought out. "The design helps us deliver and provide tangible evidence that personal service is most important," Goodine explains.

As for the future, the next logical step will see advisers becoming more mobile, using notebook computers more often, and having increasingly flexible hours to fit their clients' schedules. Although home banking, where owners could use their personal computers to handle transactions from their houses, was becoming a trend in the late 1990s, the mobile advisers give that term a new twist. This new kind of "home banking" will see St. Willibrord staff meeting with owners at home to discuss and process financial matters. There is a nice irony here. As St. Willibrord becomes more technologically advanced, it will see something of a return to the way money was handled in the 1950s when much of the credit union's business was done at people's homes.

Despite its rapid growth in the 90s, St. Willibrord has continued to set high standards for customer service. One of the attractions of many credit unions is the small-town feel and personal nature not often found at large banks. Even with more than 31,000 members, St. Willibrord still strives to provide that personal feeling. While it may not be able to match the folksy, friendly feel of its early days, St. Willibrord continues to put a great deal of emphasis on making members feel welcome, respected, and important to the overall health of the organization.

The move to relationship banking in the 90s was "a natural progression of how we could serve our members better," says Stephen Bolton, Vice-President of Branch Operations.

That dedication to service permeates the entire credit union. In addition to the overall mission statement, every branch has its own vision of how to best serve members. Then, each individual brings his or her own dedication to the task, Bolton says. The annual surveys the credit union does with its members indicate that good service continues to be appreciated. While the credit union's membership is growing, it's also increasing the amount of business each member does with it. In the past, people might have one or two accounts with St. Willibrord but then have accounts and do business with other financial institutions to handle different matters. Now, with an increased range of products and a devotion to one-on-one, more intensive service, many members are consolidating their business with the credit union. These days, a member may have a couple of accounts, a loan, a line of credit, some mutual funds and an RRSP with St. Willibrord. This is a sure sign that attention to customer service is being noticed.

Bolton admits the credit union may not always have the lowest prices and best terms, but it holds onto and attracts members because of the service provided. "Our members deal with us because of quality service. But you can't become complacent. You have to stay focused on it."

In its service agreement brochure, the credit union provides details on a Member Service Satisfaction Guarantee. The first part of it reads, "St. Willibrord is confident it will always meet or exceed the service expectation of all members in all their dealings with St. Willibrord... If a member is dissatisfied with the service received from St. Willibrord on any particular transaction or if St. Willibrord has not delivered a service in the time or in the manner promised to the member, St. Willibrord will offer, and/or the member may ask for, a full refund of any service charge or fee directly related to that transaction or service."

There are also less tangible measures of customer service. It's the way members can access senior executives, such as Jack Smit, just by calling. "When our phones ring, we pick them up and talk to our members," Bolton says. It might simply be the pleasant way a teller handles a transaction, or the way different staff members at branches get to know customers, and go out of their way to make sure the members' needs are met. It's not unusual for chocolates and other gifts to be dropped off by members for staff at Christmas time. Staff and members also share both celebrations and sad moments just as they would if they were family. It may not be what regular banking is all about, but then St. Willibrord has always been more than just a bank. To some extent, that may explain why St. Willibrord was twice, in the 1990s, voted by *London Business* magazine to be one of the 10 best places to work in the city. [See p.81] As one staff member said at that time, "The one thing that sets our company apart is... that employee opinions do count."

Jack Smit and Wilma Bastiaansen winner of the 1998 Joanne Campbell Award

One such employee who did count, and always pitched in to do whatever was needed for members, was Joanne Campbell. Following her death from cancer in 1996, the credit union decided to establish the Joanne Campbell Award for outstanding member service. Each year, a St. Willibrord employee who has gone the extra mile for members receives the award. The winners so far have been Susan Roddy (1997), Wilma Bastiaansen (1998), and Nancy Kremer (1999).

As St. Willibrord continues to grow in the next 50 years, owners will become increasingly savvy about financial matters. Bolton is confident the staff training programs initiated in the 90s and the overall dedication within the organization, which has been there since day one, will continue to make customer service an essential part of the daily business. It's no coincidence that St. Willibrord owners use the phrase, "My Credit Union", to express their relationship to the organization.

One further development to place St. Willibrord on firm financial footing was the offering of Class B Investment Shares in the credit union. The idea for selling such shares really got its start in the early 80s when the credit union was losing money and experiencing a deficit where liabilities were greater than assets. "We learned a heck of a lot from that process," says Hoevenaars now, with a laugh. "We put a lot of systems and techniques in place. Asset/liability management techniques," to reduce exposure to volatile interest rates.

The credit union began generating good profits in the late 80s and 90s, dug itself out of the deficit, and built up surplus capital. The Ministry of Finance, however, had a requirement that five per cent of total assets should be in capital, either through membership shares or retained earnings of the organization. St. Willibrord steadily built capital toward that five per cent, "but although we were making up ground, our consistently strong asset growth prevented us from making up ground fast enough," Hoevenaars explains. Until the mid-90s, credit unions in Ontario were not able to offer shares as a way of raising capital. That left St. Willibrord with the option of increasing membership shares from $50, but the increase would have had to be so substantial that it likely would have put off members. The solution came in 1994 with the new Credit Unions and Caisses Populaires Act which contained a clause allowing credit unions to raise capital above and beyond membership shares. In other words, members could voluntarily invest in the credit union. St. Willibrord had been at the forefront of getting this particular clause included in the new Act and benefited from having the NDP in power in Ontario at the time because that party had long been a supporter of credit unions.

St. Willibrord staff followed the process of getting the legislation in place and began making preparations ahead of time to produce an offering statement with specific terms and conditions.

The new Act was to be proclaimed March 1, 1995, and St. Willibrord wanted to be first out of the gate with a share offering. The Board's regular meeting was on February 28 and, as it was winding up, there were only a few minutes until midnight. Board members and senior staff waited, reviewing the new legislation, so they could officially make the decision to start the process. "We formally noted the fact that it was now March 1, and we had the legal authority to do the offering," Joosten recalls. "So we couldn't have been more than two minutes past midnight when we were taking advantage of the new legislation. We hit the ground running."

A letter was sent out to owners on March 1, calling the special General Meeting needed to adopt amendments to the Articles of Incorporation required to offer the Class B shares. It was the first credit union in Ontario to do this. Other credit unions that weren't as prepared watched with interest. St. Willibrord had studied some credit unions in B.C. that had already gone through this process and Hoevenaars notes, "We got a feel for some of the details of their share offerings."

The share offering was going to be something of a learning process for the credit union and the government, but St. Willibrord had done its homework. The administration had decided that offering $7 million in shares would be enough to meet the capital requirements. Each dollar a member invested bought a one dollar share. In order to attract members to the idea, the credit union offered an immediate 10 per cent bonus on the shares purchased. In other words, for those who invested $1,000, the credit union topped that up by another $100. To make the annual dividend attractive, St. Willibrord decided to take the monthly average of the three-to-five-year Canada Bond rate, as set by the Bank of Canada, and then add one per cent. It has turned out to be a very attractive investment.

Hoevenaars estimates it took about six months to put together the offering statement and make sure it followed every government and legal requirement. The statement was sent out to members in the early spring of 1995 with the actual issue date set for 9 a.m. on May 1. Reaction to it before May 1 was positive, and St. Willibrord management believed the shares would sell relatively quickly. To avoid having members lined up outside the branch offices on the issuing date, the administration decided that staff should come in early that day and open the offices by 7:00 a.m. "That was a bit of a concern," Hoevenaars says with a smile. "It's never good to have lineups outside financial institutions, even though this was a positive thing." Members had lots of time to mull over how much they wanted to invest (the maximum allowed was $50,000) and St. Willibrord gave them the option to cash in any other investments they had with the credit union at the time so that they could buy shares. "It was an attractive offering, we had an excellent track record of strong performance, and we had a good base of long term members who had been looking for this type of investment opportunity for a number of years," Hoevenaars recalls.

The first day of May was beautiful and sunny, welcome weather for those members who arrived at the branches at dawn. Staff in the branches had systems set up whereby, as people arrived, they could log their arrival time so that their order in the lineup was maintained. Once the doors opened, staff offered coffee and donuts to those waiting and had time to get the paperwork done before the formal issuing of shares began at 9:00 a.m. The Central Avenue administrative office was share headquarters. Staff from the branches would phone in the information from their sales sheets, and each transaction was recorded, in order, until the $7 million was bought up.

Catherine Purdy, a member of the Strathroy branch for 22 years, describes herself as, "not a morning person", but remembers getting

Lineup to purchase St. Willibrord shares May 1, 1995

to the branch office around 6:45 a.m. There were already a handful of people waiting in line, and they all signed a sheet to indicate when they arrived. When the office doors opened a few minutes later, the names were called in order for processing. There may have only been a handful when she arrived, but that number swelled significantly by the time she'd finished her transaction. Purdy remembers, "It almost reminded me of a toy store when they're selling something special and you're anticipating what's going to happen."

Bishop John Sherlock

Yvonne Brown, a London member who bought shares with her husband Alan Michael, remembers standing in line at the Central Avenue office for about an hour before the sale took place. "The atmosphere was quite exciting, and I think people were feeling pretty lucky to be inside the door. There was just sort of a fever in the air." Like most investors, she and her husband bought shares and put them into their RRSP. People had no illusions they'd be making a fortune from this offering, Brown says, "But they were feeling very confident in the credit union and wanted to express that confidence in it by buying shares."

She noticed there were many older members who had arrived early, a sign that these people who had put their faith in the credit union over the years wanted to take part in this newest offering. Bishop John Sherlock was one of the people she remembers being among the first in line. In fact, Hoevenaars recalls that having the prominent religious leader in the lineup probably allayed any fears some people might have had about making this investment. "Someone said, 'If Bishop Sherlock is investing in it then it's got to be good,'" he says. Meanwhile inside, the feeling in the Central Avenue offices was "very upbeat, a little bit tense" with all the people milling about. However, members certainly seemed to be enjoying themselves, especially those who hadn't seen each other for some time and now had a chance to catch up on the news and gossip. Although the credit union staff believed the share offering would be popular, even they didn't anticipate how fast the sale of shares would take place. "We had an exciting event going on," Hoevenaars says. "We thought it would take the morning to sell out, but as it turned out, the whole issue was sold in eleven minutes."

Perhaps no other eleven minutes in the credit union's history crystallizes the feelings and beliefs members had in the institution. A decision had been made to raise $7 million to strengthen the credit union's position for years to come and, fittingly, that money came from the people responsible for helping St. Willibrord survive and thrive into the 21st century. Since 1995, the capital raised by St. Willibrord has continued to grow. The capital portion of assets, after the sale, was over the magic five per cent and, as of September 30, 1999, had risen to 6.09 per cent.

If there were a downside to this, it was that several members had to be turned away after being told there were no shares left to purchase. This was especially felt in the Stratford branch, where the operation of share sales didn't run quite as smoothly as at the other branches. Yet Hoevenaars says he doesn't recall hearing of many hurt feelings because of the quick sales, and for now, he doesn't expect another share offering in the near future. In hindsight, he thinks the share offering would have been just as popular, and obviously less costly, if the bonus had been five per cent instead of 10. However, as the first credit union to do this in Ontario, St. Willibrord was breaking new ground.

But then, breaking new ground was nothing new to them.

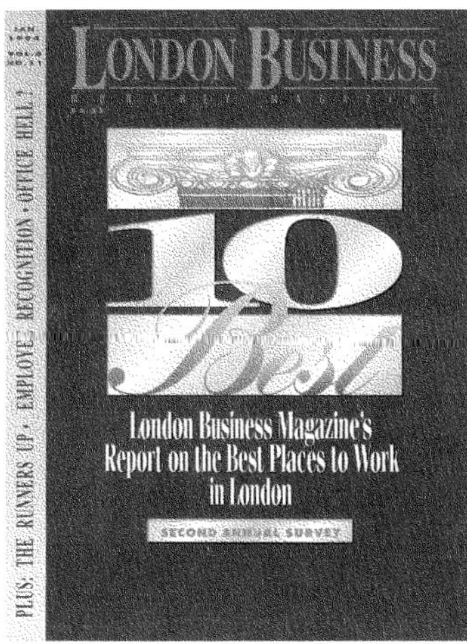

ST. WILLIBRORD COMMUNITY CREDIT UNION

NUMBER OF EMPLOYEES: 102

St. Willibrord is one of the largest credit unions in the province, providing personal and business financial services. All the customers are also members, and as such have a direct say in the management of the organization through the election of the board of directors. In business since 1951, St. Willibrord has nine branches throughout southwestern Ontario.

St. Willibrord is back again for its second year as one of the 10 best places to work in London, a feat that employees attribute to the company's on-going commitment to creating a friendly, family-like working environment, and to the respect the company shows to all employees and members.

In January of 1993, St. Willibrord moved its head office from Albert Street to 20,000 square feet of bigger and better quarters at 167 Central Avenue. The move has been good for staff morale in that it has provided a more roomy, modern work environment. The pleasant new environment was achieved with the help of all the employees, who were each given the opportunity to talk to the designers of the new office about what they would like to see incorporated in the office ergonomics.

Having the opportunity to speak their mind on an issue as important as how the new office will be laid out is just one example of the kind of communication St. Willibrord encourages between staff and management. According to Theresa Mikula, human resources manager at St. Willibrord, on-going, open communication is an essential part of creating a pleasant working environment: "The company sends out regular employee surveys," Mikula says, "and we always have excellent staff participation." According to general manager Jack Smit, the annual staff survey asks people to comment anonymously on how they are treated, how they feel about their supervisors, and if they are satisfied with their salaries and benefits.

The information generated through the survey is then shared with the company and the members through the newsletter. "The branch managers also have regular staff meetings," Smit adds, where staff are able to have direct input into how the branch is being run. "We believe very strongly in the flow of communication. We try to keep in contact."

In addition to maintaining open lines of communication, the company can also credit its on-going success to its very active staff training and performance review program. The company encourages people to advance their careers, and as long as participants receive a passing grade, the company will pay for on-going education courses. St. Willibrord prefers to promote from within, and will set up a schedule of training and education for employees that shows them which courses they should take in order to advance their careers in the direction they prefer.

The company also conducts an annual staff training day during which staff attend workshops and take part in round-table discussions on important issues. "One of the things we talked about this year," Jack Smit notes, "was why we sometimes lose members. We know what we are doing right in our business, but we also want to know what we are doing wrong."

As part of training and education, all new staff receive a full-day orientation where they learn about company policies and practices, and are told of objectives and future plans of the organization. The company's personnel objective is "To attract capable people and provide a stimulating environment for them to work and develop their careers." To hear the employees talk, the company is doing just that.

(Business London, *reprinted with permission)*

Roots &
Branches

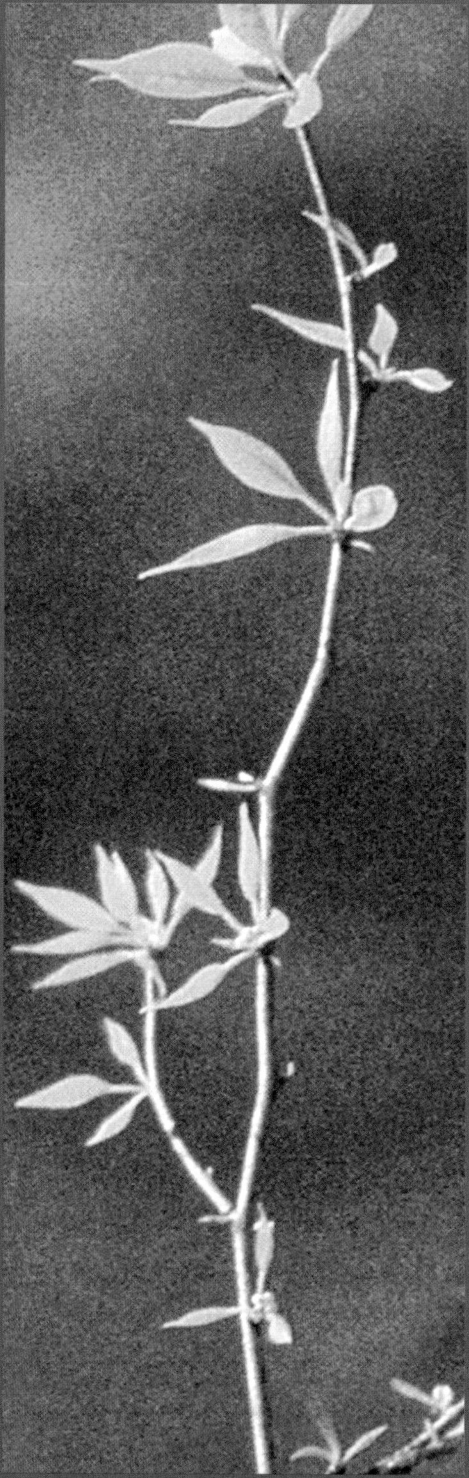

Branch
&
Administrative
Staff
2000

Back Row *(l-r): Rick Gras, Dean Brown, Ed Rychel, Mark Sarkany, John Willemse*
Middle Row *(l-r): Mia Bell, Angela Carey, Elissa DaCunha, Andrea Vossen, Marlene Keddie, Melanie Hay, Julia McIntyre, Michelle de Kort, Lisa Kennedy, Minnie Van Eyk, Henriette Demarco*
Seated *(l-r): Sandra Pella, Christy Johnson, JoAnn Pay, Sarah Van Geffen*
Absent: *Erin McMordie, Rita Vanstigt*

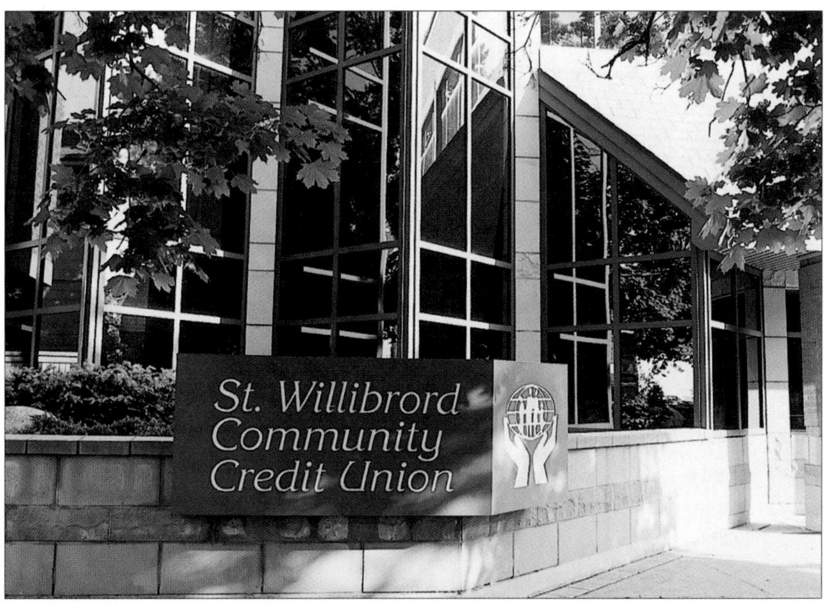

167 Central Avenue, London, Ontario

(l-r): Teresa Bakker, Jennifer Feddema, Annette Van Gorp, Ken Filson, Lia Schepers, Wilma Bastiaansen, Annette Van Dinther
Absent: *Brenda Clark, Don Duffield, Jill Van Loon*

7130 Arkona Road, Arkona, Ontario

Back Row *(l-r): Mary Anne Bell, Susan Roddy, Sharon Snow, Coby Van Reenen, Vicky Joris, Diane Leonard, Sylvia Wyant, Tilly Vandermeer, Monique Wilson*
Middle Row *(l-r): Tasha Phair, Helen Elliott, Jenny Esselment*
Seated *(l-r): Rob Eagleson, Linda Mackenzie, Shawn Robinson*
Absent: *Anne-Marie Hanna*

1315 Exmouth Street, Sarnia, Ontario

Standing *(l-r): Kimberley Emmerton, Tanya Quipp, Shirley Cook, Marilyn Koot, Julie McNeil, Jason Noble, Marty Rops, Paul Arsenault, Theresa McCall, Cheryl Leasa, Lee Ann McCaffery, Jennifer Kremkau*
Seated *(l-r): Christina Kirkpatrick, Mary Jane Chambers, Cindy Yundt, Marianne VandenHengel*

391 Huron Street, Stratford, Ontario

Standing *(l-r): Suzi French, Pauline Zimmer, Jennifer Scott, Iris Keating, Laura Koehler, Laura Walker, Pat Henderson, Tracy McGuigan, Carolyn Collins, Kim Dagenais, Jodi Mandeno*
Seated *(l-r): Dave Erskine, John DeBruyn*

11 Talbot Street West, Blenheim, Ontario

Standing *(l-r): Wanda Tupholme, Jenny Jansen, Dianne MacDougall, Patricia Pint, Fred Hackel, Joanne Vanderheyden, Ken Peters, Angela Van Bynen, Hazel McChesney, Jesse Terpstra, Michelle Van Heeswyk*
Seated *(l-r): Jackie Baxter, Ruth Skinner, Dini Leyten, Jo-Anne Beye*
Inset *(l-r): Laura McEvoy, Joyce Hurd, Marianne Kennes*

72 Front Street West, Strathroy, Ontario

Back Row *(l-r): Rita Patterson, Kathleen Mistretta, Drina Baron, Kathy Mendham, Jeff Segeren, Shelley Humphrey, Soma Persaud, Wendy McLean, Marjorie Stewart*
Middle Row *(l-r): Denise Waltham, Debbie Root, Linda Kruyssen*
Seated *(l-r): June Stevens, Jamie Campbell, Mary Voorn*
Absent: *Andrew Brown*

1867 Dundas Street East, London, Ontario

Standing *(l-r): Jennifer Caris, Pat Smits, Dave Vanos, Brenda Looman, Karey Adams*
Seated *(l-r): Nancy Kremer, Marian Rankin*
Absent*: Laura McDonald*

5307 Nauvoo Road, Watford, Ontario

Standing *(l-r): Marcy Piwowarczyk, Maria Karidas, Liz McKechnie, Stacy Fisher, Tammy Smith, Sara Lassaline, Lisa Timmers, Carla Willems*
Seated *(l-r): Penney Kerhoulas, Karen Zeleznik, Dave Dresser*
Absent: *Josie Lane, Lisa Naccarato, Nancy Van Spronsen*

841 Wellington Road South, London, Ontario

(l-r): Aaron Bickell, Cathy Orendi, Rose Klaehn, Laura Lackey, Nicole Donald

Absent: *Colleen Deloyer, Sandra Feddema*

55 Northfield Drive East, Waterloo, Ontario

Standing *(l-r): Harry Joosten, VP Owner Relations; Theresa Mikula, VP Human Resources; Frank Kennes, VP Credit*
Seated *(l-r): Stephen Bolton, VP Branch Operations; Jack Smit, President/CEO; Rick Hoevenaars, VP Finance*

Administrative Offices
167 Central Avenue, 2nd Floor, London, Ontario

Branch Supervision and Mutual Fund Administration
(l-r): Stephen Bolton, Liz McPhail, Jeanette Alsemgeest, John Adamson

Marketing and Communications, Public Affairs and Corporate Governance
Standing *(l-r): Tina Van Loon, Tania Goodine, Janet Taylor*
Seated *(l-r): Patricia Hoeksema, Harry Joosten, Jackie Westelaken*

Programming, Banking Operations, Technology and Software Support
(l-r): *Diana Jordan, Nancy Fernandes-Giles, Mary Jo Gale, Sarah Langdown, Scott Ferguson, Sheri Pittman, David Heron*
Absent: *Chris Palmer, Andrew Tennant*

Telephone Banking Services
(l-r): *Richard Czerwinski, Martha Vaughan, Tara Blake, Dawn Bayer, Barbra Unger, Kathy Mendham, Paul Ferreira*

Insurance, Pension and Estate Planning
(l-r): Cathy Hiscott, Jeanette Alsemgeest

Recruitment, Employee Training and Support, Payroll and Benefits
(l-r): Theresa Mikula, Pamela Hamilton, Patricia Devellano

Administrative and Branch Accounting, Risk Management, Treasury, Property, Trusts and Estates
Standing *(l-r): Tracy Maschke, Shannon Nolan, Sabina Graham, Teresa Ferguson, Nichole Newton*
Seated *(l-r): John de Wit, Rick Hoevenaars, Fred Blaak*
Absent: Michelle Baker

Farm, Commercial and Retail Loans and Mortgages, MemberCards, MasterCard and Merchant Administration
Standing *(l-r): Vicki Patrick, Henny Derks, Nigel Millington, Ed Boere, Frank Kennes, Roula McKiel*
Seated *(l-r): Karen Hardy, Jackie Braithwaite, Maryann LaPierre, Fiona Segeren*

Branching Out

In the early days of St. Willibrord, there were several collection points throughout the region. They could be located just about anywhere, in schools for two hours on a Friday, the church basement every Sunday after Mass, or in somebody's home. The collection points coalesced into what became known as cashiers' offices. Again, these offices were primarily part-time and informal.

Over time, cashiers' offices became known as divisions, a precursor to the branch concept, and local advisory committees came into being as well. Volunteers served on committees which were usually made up of three to five members who helped oversee the operations of the divisions. The Stratford office, for instance, was a division of St. Willibrord, and members had local annual meetings to elect their own committee which would review loan applications before they were sent to the London office for final approval by the Board loan committee. In addition, every member in all divisions was invited to the formal Annual General Meeting of the whole credit union where they participated in the election of the Board, and the credit and supervisory committees. The divisions eventually became more formalized with regular hours. Some were full-time, while others remained part-time, operating three or four days a week.

Up until the late 70s, a few of the branches were still housed in annexes to the branch managers' homes. The Chatham branch manager was Harry Wijsman, for instance, and before St. Willibrord purchased the Blenheim Credit Union, that office was annexed to Wijsman's house. In Stratford, the office was an annex at the front of José Cozyn's house until a new office was built in the early 1980s. In most cases, the credit union paid rent to the managers for leasing approximately 500 sq. ft., a payment separate from the salary paid to the managers. There were some exceptions. In Stratford, a port-a-vault with teller lockers and a small group of safety deposit boxes was installed in the manager's home, a feature for which St. Willibrord paid directly. In Sarnia, the credit union owned the manager's house, and rather than pay the manager to rent the office space, the manager paid rent to the credit union on the residential portion.

St. Willibrord was the first credit union in Ontario to establish this type of branch network in order to serve its membership. As Jack Smit notes, the foundation for the branch concept dates back to the very early days of the credit union when the various divisions held separate annual meetings, rather than holding just one annual meeting for the whole group. "The branches also established advisory committees which, although elected, weren't formally recognized by legislation or the bylaws. Inevitably, the Board started consulting with these committees whenever there was a major decision to be made."

The advisory committees provided the vehicle through which the credit union decentralized its operations. John Strybosch notes that even though there were not that many people involved yet, "It was suggested that we should have a system of delegates [to attend the Annual General Meeting] in order to ensure that all the branches were fairly represented, regardless of the actual size of the branch." The concern expressed by Strybosch was that without a system of delegates, it might be possible for one particular group to make decisions that affected, but were not backed by, other groups. "For instance, there might be 110 members attending the Annual General Meeting. Of these, maybe only 20 to 30 would be from outside the city of London where the meeting was held. If the local majority decided they wanted a particular member elected to the Board, the outlying branches would be unable to prevent them." The delegate system would make certain that representation at meetings would be more equitable. Even so, it was not until 1982 that the branches elected delegates instead of sending members to the Annual General Meeting.

Each branch was allocated a minimum of seven delegate positions, regardless of the branch's actual membership. The agreement was that there would be 100 delegates in total. With the six branches of that time, that accounted for the first 42 positions.

The other 58 positions were allocated on the basis of each branch's proportion of the total membership. If a given branch had 20 percent of the members, they received 20 percent of the remaining delegate positions. There was also a provision in the bylaws that no branch, regardless of size, would ever have more than 49 delegates.

The delegate system remains intact, with the exception of the later removal of alternates, and expansion in 1997 to 120 delegate positions. Before then, each branch was allowed to elect two or three alternative delegates who would attend the Annual General Meeting if another delegate couldn't make the meeting. The alternate delegate system was removed to simplify the elections and promote the attendance of appointed delegates at the meetings.

In addition to encouraging communication between administration and the branches, the duties of the advisory committees, which eventually grew into the more formalized branch councils, included receiving monthly branch reports, offering advice on various aspects of branch operations, and advising on land acquisitions or approving loan applications. The committees would also conduct year-end cash counts on behalf

NAMES AND PLACES

As early as 1951, several branches of the credit union were organized and additional ones followed in subsequent years. In the course of the first twenty-five years, branches were operative in Windsor, Wallaceburg, Wyoming, Strathroy, Seaforth, and Woodstock. Variations were implemented involving changes of location and amalgamation. At present, there are ten branches of St. Willibrord Community Credit Union.

Over the years, the names given to branches evolved from "Afdelingen", through "Subdivisions", and "Divisions", to "Branches". The managers, originally titled cashiers, are now branch managers. They are also loan officers in accordance with existing legal provisions.

In addition to the large Annual General Meeting for representatives of all branches, there are yearly meetings of the members at the branch level which provide an opportunity for them to associate with each other in the credit union spirit, serve the purposes of financial reporting, elections, information, and encouragement regarding credit union services.

of the external auditor and, in general, serve to promote the credit union.

By establishing the branches, St. Willibrord was, in many respects, decentralizing its authority. This action was furthered by the appointment of branch managers. Although St. Willibrord encouraged consistency throughout the organization, managers introduced distinctive managerial styles during their tenures. But the decentralized model has worked well for the credit union. The arrangement with the members was essentially that the local committees were elected, and if they made unpopular decisions, they would not last long in office. The decentralized model did mean that the overall structure was not as efficient as a smaller, tighter organization might have been, but major decisions were not made unless there was substantial support from the membership.

The Board has often felt that the branches are indeed so decentralized and autonomous that they almost constitute franchises rather than units of the whole. But that is perceived as good because management wants local staff to have an entrepreneurial spirit, while still using the St. Willibrord model with respect to pricing and policies. How the services and products are delivered remains very much up to the branches. This decentralized model has proven itself time and again, and is one of the things that attracted the Kingswood Credit Union of Kitchener to St. Willibrord in 1998. They knew they could join St. Willibrord, enjoy economies of scale, but still retain their sense of being part of the local community.

As St. Willibrord grows, the model of keeping the branches semi-autonomous, while still holding a common corporate vision and philosophy, is likely to continue. It is a model that has worked since the very first cashiers delivered basic, financial services out of their homes or the local church, and it is a model that continues to be appreciated by an increasingly diverse membership.

London Downtown

The London Downtown branch is the oldest of ten St. Willibrord branches because it is successor to the original single office. While St. Willibrord was located at 150 Kent Street, and for the first few years at 151 Albert Street, banking and administrative functions of the credit union were still combined. When the organization moved to the Albert Street location, a block away from the Kent Street office, Martin Verbeek was manager of the credit union, a function which was not yet distinct from the London Downtown branch manager's role.

Administrative and branch management responsibilities of the office were not formally divided until the Albert Street building had a second storey added in November 1976, although the plan to separate branch service from overall management functions had been in place for about a year. It was decided to move the administrative staff of St.Willibrord upstairs, and establish a separate owner service facility on the main floor with Wally Mutsaers as branch manager. At the same time, a London branch advisory committee was reconstituted to operate separately from the Board of Directors.

Although not initially thought of as a branch, per se, the tradition of having a banking facility attached to the administration continued after the creation of the new offices on Central Avenue, establishing what was, in effect, a main, or central, branch.

Mutsaers did not remain as branch manager of this office very long because the former Co-op Services joined with St. Willibrord in October 1977, adding a new branch to the network. Shortly thereafter, Mutsaers became the manager of that office on Wharncliffe Road South in London. He remained so after the branch was moved to its new home on Dundas Street East in 1980, and continued as branch manager until his retirement in 1998.

Camiel DeVries served as branch manager from 1978 to 1980. Jack Smit was acting branch manager for nine months, and then Jim Wincott served from 1981 until February 1993.

In 1993, John Willemse became manager at the London Downtown branch. Willemse had served as branch manager in Arkona from 1971 until 1987, serving also as manager of the Sarnia branch from 1971 to 1974. In 1987, he returned to Sarnia as manager until taking up his duties at London Downtown, a tenure that lasted until April of 1998 when he decided to take on the less-onerous responsibilities of account manager in anticipation of his retirement.

Since its creation, London Downtown has had a slightly different status from the other branches because of its proximity to the administration. Although every effort is made to function independently from the head office, the very fact that it is physically located below the administrative offices means that it has easier access to management, and it is also under closer scrutiny. The responsibilities of managing the branch fell to Ed Rychel in April of 1998, and he is clear that, although the London Downtown branch

At the public ceremony celebrating construction of the Central Avenue building, now home to the London Downtown branch and the Administrative offices, April 27, 1992

(Above) *Then Mayor Tom Gosnell and Deputy Mayor Dianne Haskett add their "city approval" piece to the giant jigsaw puzzle symbolizing the process which led to the successful completion of 167 Central Avenue*
(Below) *The completed puzzle with all pieces in place so that a new building could be ready to serve St. Willibrord and its many owners*

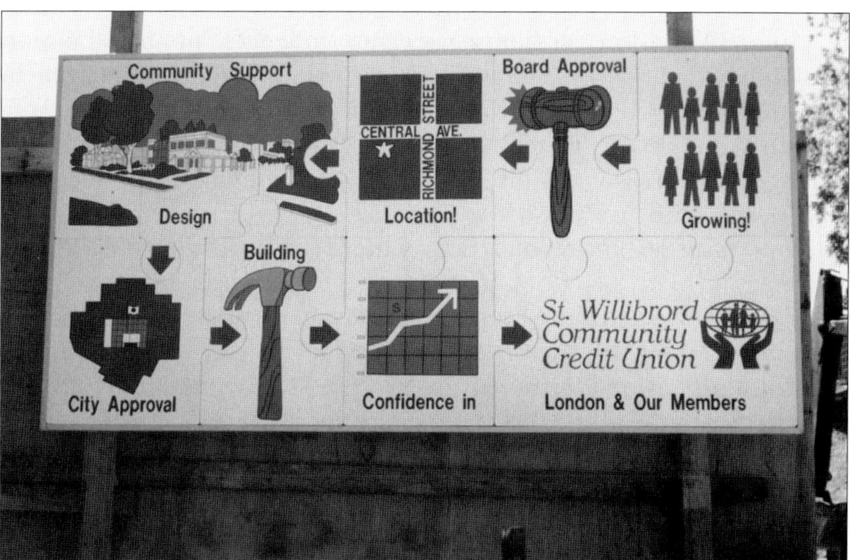

of the credit union is housed in the same building as the administrative offices, the branch is a separate entity entirely. "Our functions and services are the same as in the other branches," he says. "We serve a slightly different clientele, perhaps, in that we have more commercial owner/members than the other branches." The kinds of commercial accounts at London Downtown range from those for individual entrepreneurs to large corporations, and law firms. "We have a large number of builders as well who bank here," he adds, "but we are probably not too different from other branches when it comes to the individuals we serve." As of May 2000, there were 4,840 owners at the London Downtown branch, which had the largest number of staff of all the branches at 22. "But we are the second largest branch after Strathroy," he notes. "I considered it part of my mission, when I came on board, to make this branch the largest, and I am confident we will achieve that."

Before coming to St. Willibrord, Rychel worked at another financial institution for 18 years, and has found that the level of technology in use at the credit union surpasses any he had seen elsewhere. He also believes that the owner/members at St. Willibrord take to the use of technology with enthusiasm. "The central branch came second only after Strathroy in the number of people who signed up for the on-line banking services between April and June of 1999." Getting more owners to use technology is one of the goals for London Downtown in 2000 and beyond.

Most marketing campaigns are credit union wide, but each branch has the responsibility for developing its own business plan for each year, and marketing initiatives are included in that business plan. Like the other branches, London Downtown does some brainstorming with senior management around what marketing strategies might be successful, and then initiates the plans that are selected. Rychel observes, "What is happening on an increasing level is that there are a lot of ideas out there, and I think these ideas should be shared among all the branches, and not be applied to just one branch." The credit union has an annual growth target of 10 per cent. Plans in the works for 2000 and beyond include an active promotion of the MeritLines®, and the IdeaLoans®, and targeting owners in the age range of 18 to 21 years old with a MasterCard® campaign, in an effort to encourage these owners to obtain these cards before they enter university or college. "We also plan to let sports and charitable organizations know that they can use our boardroom for their meetings. We plan to increase our involvement with the community."

Arkona

Because of the credit union's rural roots, Arkona collection points, and later the branch offices there, have played an important part in the development of St. Willibrord almost from the start.

In the credit union's early days, Arkona was something of a central catchment for area farms stretching from Strathroy to Grand Bend. When John Strybosch moved to Arkona in the 1960s, the small branch in his home took on a more vital role as a place where area farmers could come and deposit their money or seek out a loan.

Peter Van Engelen, who came to Canada from the Netherlands in 1953, settled in Thedford to operate a dairy farm with his brother. Van Engelen became member number 754 and, within a year, was on the local committee evaluating loan applications and dealing with any other business of the credit union in the area. The credit union was more likely to provide loans to Dutch newcomers than a bank would, he recalls, but it was frustrating that there wasn't more money available in those early days to help farmers expand more quickly. "In a credit union that small, it was not easy for farmers who wanted to expand to borrow the money," so they often would have to approach a local bank, too.

Jack Boere

Wilma Bastiaansen (née Caris) left the Netherlands with her family in 1961 and, by the following year, she had made the acquaintance of the Strybosch family and soon had a job at the credit union in London. Three years later, however, Strybosch had bought a doctor's home/office in Arkona and was using it as the office for the bookkeeping business he started with Bastiaansen's brother, the late Matthew Caris. It only made sense that it serve as a credit union office too. On November 1, 1964, the new Arkona division was opened with John Strybosch as cashier. It was St. Willibrord's second office, after London, to offer full-time service to members, and within six months Bastiaansen was an employee there. "I transferred to Arkona in March 1965," Bastiaansen recalls. "I worked at John's house. We had the front living room for our credit union office; then when the doctor moved out, John used that office for his business."

The Arkona office was open five days a week. Collection points

Arkona branch office, 1964-75

were still available at sub-offices in Grand Bend, and the Forest area was served, for some time, by the late Jack Boere from his home in Forest. Collection for the Wyoming area was done by Boere in the basement of a church. Eventually, Forest and Wyoming merged with Arkona and from there, Boere served his members. The Grand Bend collections were made every Wednesday afternoon in an old house the credit union was able

Wilma Bastiaansen, 1967

to rent for only $100 a year. The house was full of flies, bees and every other insect imaginable, and credit union staff sometimes had to take fuel with them to heat the house in the winter time. Despite the primitive conditions, area farmers conducted their business there each week. It wasn't until September of 1976 that the Grand Bend operation was closed. By then, most members from that area were already dealing directly with the Arkona branch.

On Friday evenings, through the late 1960s, Bastiaansen or Strybosch would head to Strathroy to do credit union transactions at Our Lady Immaculate Separate School. Saturday afternoons, in Watford, when livestock and vegetable sales were taking place in the village, they'd handle accounts at St. Peter Canisius Separate School. "So people who were going to the sale sold a cow and then, right away, came to us with their money," she notes.

During the 1960s, the Arkona operation had a formal office, and transactions were kept on ledger cards with account numbers to record the deposits and withdrawals. Bastiaansen remembers handling about 10 cheques a day and keeping up to $2,500 in cash before sending it on to the London office. These were the days of IOUs in the drawer, and a cashbox that was stuffed under Strybosch's bed each night. When the story is brought up of the time Strybosch's then-young son took money from the cashbox one day to pass out bills to school chums, Bastiaansen laughs. "You know, I didn't find out about that until about seven years ago. I wasn't aware of it then."

It was a time when all members were still Dutch or Flemish, and much of the business was done in a variety of Dutch dialects, she recalls. "My Mum used to be able to tell, at night when I got home, which people I'd been dealing with that day because I would pick up some of their dialect."

Like much of the credit union business back then, socializing and trust were big parts of the operation. You didn't just come and deposit money, but spent time chatting, getting caught up on the local news, or sharing stories about your family. "Somebody would come in to make a deposit and John would open the kitchen door, then call to his wife, 'Lena, bring a coffee please.' She usually had squares and cookies to go with that."

Van Engelen remembers that local committee meetings would last for hours, just as much for socializing as for the business at hand. "When the meeting was over, well, everything was new to us, so we talked about a lot of things. It was one or two o'clock in the morning before I'd get home. We had a nice social talk with a cup of coffee."

And as Bastiaansen recalls, during office hours she and Strybosch would always go the extra step to keep members happy. "We did whatever needed to be done. One day, a fellow brought in a box with all kinds of bills, and we had to sort this out. I got tired of reaching into that box so I dumped it on the desk and there was a nest of mice," she remembers with a laugh. "I'm not very fond of mice. Or a member would bring in a bucketful of loose change. Member service! Take it and roll it with a smile."

Bastiaansen also helped Dutch members book trips back home, and continued to do so when she left the credit union for several years to raise a family. She received five dollars a trip. As an example of how St. Willibrord staff does the little extras for members, she still helps some older members fill out their Dutch pension forms on her own time.

Like any other branch, there was a committee set up to deal with loan applications, for example, and that didn't always sit well with prospective members. Some farmers didn't like the idea of their neighbours knowing how much money they had or wanted to borrow. The key to building up trust was to "keep your mouth shut" so that word about people's financial situation didn't hit the street, Van Engelen recalls. And there was concern that a neighbour on the committee would be the one deciding whether you got money or not. "But sometimes we gave people a loan because they were good enough farmers and we knew they would pay it back. So you had to know the people." It may have been a more informal way of doing business, but today's thriving branch is a testament to the commitment to the credit union of people like Van Engelen. "It was an experience," he says. "Well, I think we did a pretty good job for the time. And I thought if you could help people, that was something I enjoyed too."

Through the 1970s, the credit union continued to grow in Arkona and increasingly took on more sophistication. But until recent years, most of the business funnelled through the London head office, and communications weren't as sophisticated then as they are now. Bastiaansen remembers how she would exchange mail and records in those days. "The manager of the Sarnia branch was also the manager of London for a while. He would come along Highway 22 to go to Sarnia and we lived just off Highway 22. I met him after work, at the highway, to exchange paperwork at a pre-established time. It might be a loan application or other paperwork because there was no fax or e-mail then, and regular mail was not always fast enough."

John Willemse took over as manager in Arkona in 1971, still working out of Strybosch's old home. A teller's station had been built in the entranceway, and behind it was the interview office for handling other credit union business. Willemse's background was in retail sales, but Strybosch had convinced him to try the credit union for a year. It was a move that paid off. That one-year trial turned into a career since Willemse stayed as branch manager in Arkona until 1987. (He held the same post in Sarnia for six years, and then in the London Downtown branch office.) When he looks back at his days in Arkona, he remembers how little he knew about the credit union in the first months. "Fortunately, I had a good rapport with John [Strybosch]," Willemse recalls. "He made a comment once that he had never had anybody who had more questions than I did. That was likely because my background wasn't in the financial field." He remembers Strybosch separating out the different documents needed to process the particular kinds of loans the credit union offered, and then Willemse was on his own. But he learned quickly because Arkona became the credit union's most profitable branch at that time. Working with teller Marian Rankin (née Van Loon), he gained more knowledge about the business, and eventually the Strathroy and Watford branches (where Rankin transferred) grew out of the Arkona operation. Nevertheless, the Arkona branch at that point was still relatively small, and although Willemse was also responsible for managing the Sarnia branch, he had time to develop new business and help both operations grow quickly in the 70s. "My main legacy will be in the Arkona area, building that branch. Those three branches - Arkona, Strathroy, and Watford - are the triangle. To me, they've always been the heart of the credit union and still are today."

The turning point in the Arkona branch's history came in July 1975, when they moved into new headquarters just outside the village and across from Taxandria Club, a Dutch-Canadian meeting place which Strybosch had helped found. Van Engelen says the new office was important to the branch, but he would have liked it closer to the heart of the village. Unfortunately, there wasn't any location available at the right price and with enough parking spaces. "We had to go with what we could find, and so we built it across from Taxandria," Van Engelen says. "But I always thought it would be better in the centre of Arkona."

Still, it meant no more meeting in cramped quarters in a house, and the new office was so modern and spacious that the credit union only used half the building at first. Today, St. Willibrord has the building all to itself. There's an openness and flow to the interior that makes it easy to carry on conversations among staff and members who drop in. The trust and informality that existed in the early days is still a part of the Arkona operation. Members are just as likely to drop in and see manager Annette Van Dinther (née Van Loy) as to make a formal appointment.

"The people who work here live in the community," says Van Dinther. "I've lived here all my life, so there are very few times that someone walks in and I don't know who they are. If I'm not busy, I'll make a point of saying 'Hi' to people, and the rest of the staff does that too."

Owner Bob Vaughan with Manager Annette Van Dinther, March 2000

Membership growth at the branch runs at about four or five per cent annually, most of it coming from word-of-mouth as people seek an alternative to banks. With automated services and telephone banking, the Arkona branch has members as far away as Tillsonburg, and Bayfield. While the branch is known for its relaxed, informal atmosphere, it still has a sophistication, particularly in the agricultural sector of banking, that makes it popular.

"We focus on agriculture here because of the location we're in," says Van Dinther who runs a farm in the area with her husband. "We have strong agricultural backgrounds so we understand what members are talking about when they discuss their farm operation. And members tell us we have a lot more personal service even with approvals for loans. That it doesn't have to go to Toronto for approval, but instead is done within the area is a big plus."

The branch handles a number of commercial accounts from businesses in Arkona and beyond, and Van Dinther would like to see an increase in consumer wage earners as members. "But this is the heart of agriculture. That's our focus and where our strengths will stay. And I think we have some opportunities to see real increases."

One drawback to the branch was that it was seen by some as more of a training centre for other St. Willibrord employees. Many staff did receive their start at the Arkona branch but then moved on

Annette Van Dinther congratulates owner Carolyn Michaelson, grand prize winner of the "Bright Ideas" contest (Adult Division), January 2000

to other branches in larger municipalities. However, it also meant that staff who remained, loved living in the area, and this created long-term relationships with members.

Trying to get younger owners is also a challenge, as people out of school often have difficulty finding jobs in the area and move elsewhere to pursue a career. Van Dinther hopes, however, that those young, mobile owners link up, eventually, with branches of St. Willibrord that are located in cities where jobs may be more plentiful.

As one of the branches awarded the credit union's Five Star performance designation in the past four years, Arkona has shown it is a shining star in the St. Willibrord firmament. "I think the atmosphere of this branch is special because it's small, friendly, and we go out of our way to talk to our members," says Van Dinther. "I think it's a focus we've always had in this branch, and I'm sure it will continue."

SARNIA

Linda Mackenzie remembers an elderly couple who joined St. Willibrord a few years ago. They were disenchanted with past relationships they'd had with other financial institutions and appeared to distrust what the credit union could offer them. But the manager of the Sarnia branch and her staff went to work to convince the couple that St. Willibrord was different. They made home visits, focused on personal service, and even sent the couple flowers.

Today, it's not uncommon to see the same couple coming into the branch smiling, hugging their financial services representative, and handling their money with confidence. "They look forward to their visits," Mackenzie says.

It's this personal approach that has made the Sarnia branch a strong member of the St. Willibrord family. Like other branches, Sarnia has evolved tremendously in recent years and offers services to members that were only dreamed of a decade or two ago. Today, there's a wealth of financial products available, but the one thing that hasn't changed is the personal touch that tells member/owners they're important. "People who join still comment on the friendliness of the staff, the atmosphere, and how everything is so personable," says Coby Van Reenen, a financial service assistant at the branch.

Sharon Snow, Financial Service Assistant

Not only is Sarnia now one of the more successful branches, it's also one of the oldest. A Sarnia area division has existed within the credit union since September 16, 1951, less than a year after St. Willibrord was founded. For many years afterward, the Sarnia branch operated like others outside London, with business transactions taking place around the kitchen table of someone's house and people catching up on the news and gossip when they came to make deposits or talk about loans.

Coby Van Reenen, Financial Service Assistant

John Van Werde, who's been involved with the credit union for some 30 years, remembers earlier days. Van Werde had lived in Canada for about five years before he joined St. Willibrord. He recalls the meetings and banking that went on in former manager Martin Verbeek's home on Claxton Street, appreciating the friendly and personal atmosphere. He's watched the branch grow over the years, notably in March 1972 when a new office at 1177 Pontiac Drive was purchased, and the years afterward when John Willemse was doing double duty managing both the Arkona and Sarnia branches.

John Van Werde, former Sarnia branch council member and 30 year owner

In those days, Sarnia members borrowed money for cars and other goods, as opposed to the Arkona branch where loans were mainly for livestock and farm equipment purchases. Because of the growth years in the 1970s, a new branch office was opened in May 1979 at 1315 Exmouth Street, and it remains the Sarnia headquarters today. "The growth has been very positive," says Van Werde. "There's very good management, and they're doing an excellent job and providing more services."

John Willemse left Arkona in May 1987 to manage the Sarnia branch full time and further increase its potential. Prior to his arrival, Fred Rusticus had served as manager from 1974 to 1980, and Hans Maas managed the branch between 1980 and 1987. When John Willemse left Sarnia in 1993, after a prosperous beginning to the 90s, he was succeeded by Nigel Millington who also managed during a strong growth period from May 1993 to 1997. Linda Mackenzie became manager in July of 1997 and saw, in 1997-98 alone, growth of 24 per cent over the previous year. There were more than 2,590 members, and Portfolio Totals, as of May 2000, of $108 million. Portfolio Totals represent Total Deposits+Loans+Mutual Fund Balances under administration.

Coby Van Reenen and Susan Roddy, a financial adviser, have been at the branch since 1983 and know that this prosperity didn't come quickly. Roddy recalls her early days at the branch as quiet. "I can remember that some of the tellers would sit and do needlepoint in the middle of the day." Van Reenen laughs, telling how someone danced on a desk one day, and how staff brought in books and magazines to pass the time. She also remembers that most of the members at the time she joined St. Willibrord were either Dutch Catholic, or Dutch Christian Reformed. "They felt very at home. And most of the people who worked here spoke Dutch, so that made them more comfortable."

Even though the Exmouth office was relatively new when Roddy

Susan Roddy, Financial Adviser, with Pauline and Arnold Rockx, Account Holders Number 59

and Van Reenen started, staff only used half the building and were crammed for space. Van Reenen remembers one teller who was pregnant. When she had to pull out her cash drawer, she had to sit on the desk behind her to have enough room to operate. Of course, no one could get by until the teller finished the transaction. Still, staff had fun. Members would drop by on a whim to chat, one of whom would bring soup with meatballs when staff were working late.

But it was a time when St. Willibrord offered fewer services and staff didn't go after business as proactively as they do now. "I think for a long time there was a perception from people in the community that credit unions were very limited in what they could do. They didn't realize we were a full financial service," Van Reenen says. Mackenzie adds, "We weren't seen as much of a competitive threat back then. But now, we're a bit of a thorn to banks."

Fortunately, the good feelings among the staff and members still exist. Employees talk about how they enjoy coming to work, that

Jacqui Lee, young owner, with Jenny Esselment, Financial Service Representative

they mesh together as a team, and work well with the local branch council. Van Reenen believes members notice this feeling, are quick to share personal stories, and show recent family photos.

With its long and storied past, the Sarnia branch looks forward to the future with confidence. Mackenzie wants to see an all-inclusive banking relationship with members where they combine both their personal and business financial needs at the credit union. She sees the branch getting bigger and better in the next few years, including adding space to the existing office to meet demand for services. "We expect to physically grow in membership, yes. And we haven't even begun to tap the resources in this city, especially with commercial clients."

Like other branches, Sarnia can offer its members Internet and phone banking, which means people throughout Lambton County are using the branch. Retirees who spend part of the year in Florida can still deal financially with St. Willibrord, and there's even a member in Singapore who banks electronically.

In the end, however, future success will depend on what's always

Shawn Robinson, Service Representative, with Taylor Hamilton, young owner

been here - personal service. Roddy notes, "We want to build a strong relationship with people. It's all about building that trust."

Owners appreciate that staff members have been there long term, know their needs, and are willing to listen. While automated banking is a good added service, it can't replace the personal contact owners want. "They can ask the questions to a person. They can't ask a bank machine about products or concerns," Mackenzie adds. "If you've got a good relationship, and they trust your advice, they're going to stay here. I think there is great potential for growth, but we can't lose that personal service."

Stratford

José Cozyn remembers clearly the days when she was cashier of the Stratford branch of St. Willibrord Community Credit Union and ran the office out of her small home on Blake Street, a home built during the Second World War and commonly referred to as a "wartime" house. "My office was my kitchen table," she recalls. "The children were small then, and were trained to be quiet if somebody dropped by on credit union business. We only had the one TV, and when people came, the kids would hide behind the couch so they could still see their show but not disturb the visitors." That was in 1969, when Cozyn became the first woman cashier of a St. Willibrord credit union branch, a position she would hold, with the title of branch manager, until her retirement in 1994.

But before Cozyn accepted the position of cashier, the survival of the Stratford branch had been a far from certain thing. Created in early 1953, after a meeting held in the home of Peter Leyser on Caledonia Street in Stratford, where several people had expressed a desire for a local branch, an office was opened on March 15 of that year in the home of Mr. Leyser. Jan DeJong, Jules DeBrabandere, Ysbrand Boersen, Leo Tovenatti, and Peter Leyser were installed as the advisory committee. The members of the advisory committee were able to act as collectors of deposits, but only the cashier could accept loan applications.

In 1958, Gerard Van Leeuwen was appointed to the position of cashier, and for three years the office was located on his farm in Easthope Township. When he resigned in 1961, the position was given to Peter French who subsequently resigned after only serving a few months in order to accept a job relocation. Gerry Nyenhuis became cashier in January of 1962, and the office moved to Birmingham Street back in Stratford.

Because the Stratford membership had grown considerably during the past decade, with members as far away as Lucknow, Ontario, more than 110 km (70 miles) away, another office was opened in Seaforth with Harry Hak as cashier.

In 1965, Nyenhuis resigned as cashier, handing the responsibilities to Leo Savelberg who took over the reins in January 1966. The branch office was located in the basement of his home.

By 1967, there were 190 members of the Stratford branch. Mr. William Van Westerop was elected secretary to the advisory committee, and for the first time in the branch's history, the minutes of the Stratford division were recorded in English rather than Dutch.

When John Strybosch became general manager of St. Willibrord in 1969, he initiated a number of administrative changes to the operation of the credit union, intended to streamline operations and cut costs. Savelberg disagreed with some of these changes, and closed the Stratford office in August 1969. This left the members with no option but to go to the London or the Seaforth office to conduct their business.

Jack DeGroot, known to his friends as Jake, was chairman of the Stratford committee, and he felt very strongly that the Stratford office should be resurrected. After winning the support of the Board of Directors by a single vote, he initiated a search for a replacement for Savelberg. José Cozyn remembers the day she received a call from DeGroot wanting to talk to her about the possibility of taking on the responsibility. At the time, Cozyn was secretary of the Benelux Club in Stratford, a club devoted to the interests of people from Belgium, the Netherlands, and Luxembourg. "Jake was a man of very few words," she recalls, "but meant what he said when he spoke. So he came to see me, told me he was looking for someone to take over as cashier, and said, 'You've got space in your front room here. You could easily do it.'"

Jack (Jake) DeGroot

"I had two kids back then," Cozyn says, "and had just started to work again in a half-day job at a brokerage firm, and wasn't sure I wanted to take on this responsibility. But Jake, John Strybosch and Wally Mutsaers came down on the Friday of a Labour Day weekend to talk to me, and John was talking about all the changes that he was planning for the credit union, none of which meant very much to me as I was not familiar with the way things had been done before. But

Stratford Branch Grand Opening, 1984

Jake was getting concerned, and at one point said, "Don't paint the picture so bleak, John. She'll never accept!"

Cozyn was convinced to accept the position of cashier for a six month probationary period, and on Tuesday following the long weekend, she opened her doors for business. The Stratford branch had narrowly escaped being permanently closed. However, it remained open because of the determined efforts of Jake DeGroot, the vision of John Strybosch, and the willingness of José Cozyn to take on the responsibilities of running the office.

For the next 25 years, Cozyn ran the Stratford branch, first relocating to an old Lands and Forests building at 430 Huron Street, a busy highway coming into town. That new office had plenty of parking, and offered easy access to rural members of the credit union.

José Cozyn's retirement dinner, 1994

Then, in 1982, with a growing number of members and an increasing assortment of services and products, it became clear that new accommodations would have to be found for the office. It was decided that, in spite of the recession, land should be bought and a proper office constructed. When property across the street from the existing office became available, the credit union bought it and constructed its current offices.

"At first, we didn't quite know what to do with all that space," notes Cozyn. "It was quite an adjustment moving from 500 square feet of space into this large, modern office complex."

Since her retirement in 1994, José has concentrated her efforts on helping her husband run Cozyn's Garden Gallery. She often visits the branch, and still misses her interaction with credit union members and the staff at the office. But she takes pride in her accomplishments while she had responsibility for the branch.

Marty Rops is the current branch manager, and he foresees considerable change for both the branch and the credit union in

Young Owners

Tommy Kelly

Rachel and Stacey Koot

Casey Williamson

general. Along with major renovations to the current office building, Rops predicts that the credit union will offer more technology-based services to its members. "Home banking seems to be one of the things that owners really want, and I anticipate that will be one of the more significant changes we will see in the near future. People will want to do more of their banking over the Internet." As Rops points out, society is increasingly moving towards cashless transactions. "People will use money cards instead of cash," he notes. But he also adds that there will always be some credit union members who want to maintain the personal touch that has set the credit union apart from banks. "As long as there are people who prefer to do their business in person, we will be here to serve them."

Blenheim

Since 1952, people in the Chatham/Blenheim area have been served by St. Willibrord Community Credit Union. Over the years, they've had to do business in a variety of locations: an insurance office in Chatham, a corner shop on Blenheim's main street, a space at Kent County Fertilizer, and a farm office on a side-road between the two municipalities. Today, a large and modern building in Blenheim is home to the branch.

Harry Wijsman, who emigrated from the Netherlands in 1949, has been at the centre of the branch's history for most of those years, starting out as a collector in the 1950s and eventually becoming a full-time employee with St. Willibrord in 1973. Now retired, Wijsman remembers those early days fondly. "People came in with five dollars, three dollars. They never came in with cheques; it was always cash. Everything was trust."

Harry Wijsman

Like many of the credit union's branches, Blenheim was built mostly on the prosperity of area farmers. In the early days, the local branch council would process loan applications to be handled by the main office in London, but Wijsman remembers it was mostly for "small stuff" such as appliances, furniture, and possibly some farm equipment. Banks in those days had little interest in lending even minor amounts to small business people and farmers, while finance companies charged more than 20 per cent interest on money they lent. The credit union, which used to charge one per cent interest per month on unpaid balances, was ideally placed in the middle ground and steadily grew because of it, Wijsman recalls. "Word of mouth was the best way to grow. People would come by [to my office] and chat. They didn't come for banking; they came for a visit. A lot of people would just come in to see me."

John DeBruyn, now the branch manager, remembers coming as a child with his father to see Wijsman when he had a corner office operation in Blenheim that was opened after church on Sundays. DeBruyn's father spent a lot of time socializing while the kids waited in the car, anxious to get on with the day. That was typical of the informal nature of doing business back then.

Wijsman, like other pioneers from the credit union's early history, did much of this work for no pay. That changed in the 1960s, and he remembers asking that his fee be paid in one lump sum near Christmas, so that he'd have much-appreciated cash for gifts. In 1973, when his first wife died, Wijsman had to choose between running his farm full-time and taking a regular job with St. Willibrord. Manager John Strybosch convinced him to choose the latter, and the next few years would see some of the most significant changes in the branch's history.

Another credit union had been operating in Blenheim for many years, starting out in St. Mary's Parish, and then becoming the Blenheim Credit Union. John Cowan, who worked for many years at that credit union, said it was small and not growing much by the late 1970s. The amount of business and service it could provide its members was limited, and like other small credit unions of the day, faced extinction if it couldn't grow. St. Willibrord representatives, including Wijsman, began talking with Cowan and others about a merger. Blenheim Credit Union members resisted at first because they were proud of the organization they had built and didn't want to see it end. Like St. Willibrord, it had started out as a small, Catholic credit union, which meant the two did have a few things in common. "It took a hell of a long time to convince them," Wijsman remembers, but on January 2, 1980, St. Willibrord purchased the Blenheim Credit Union, merged it with its then Chatham branch, and in May moved into new headquarters on Blenheim's main street. The credit union had to do about $60,000 worth of renovations to bring the building up to standard, and rented the space for the next 10 years. Not all the Blenheim Credit Union members chose to stay with St. Willibrord, but some of its movers and shakers, like Cowan, joined the local branch council and worked hard to make the new operation work.

Signing the purchase and sale agreement with Blenheim Community Credit Union
(Seated l-r) *Ann Westelaken, Bill Intven*
(Standing l-r) *Claire Taylor, John Féron*

The early 1980s were slow growth times for the Blenheim branch, and Wijsman and Cowan recall a few local members wondering if the "new kid on the block" would survive. Wijsman soon wanted a new manager in Blenheim and thought of DeBruyn. He suggested him to St. Willibrord's administration, but much to Wijsman's chagrin, DeBruyn was hired to work for a year in London. By 1983, however, DeBruyn had come back to Kent County and ended up getting first-hand knowledge of all the branch business from being a teller to handling loans. It wasn't fun at first, but "in hindsight it was good, because I learned the process of the entire credit union operation," DeBruyn now says.

Fortunately, as the decade moved forward, business in Blenheim picked up. Some old habits of several members such as not depositing cheques at the credit union, even though that service had been offered for years, also died out. "They used to go to the bank, cash the cheques and then bring the money down here," says Wijsman, shaking his head. "It took years, but finally people started recognizing us as a financial institution, and realized we were here to stay."

The Blenheim branch had taken out two five-year leases on the building, but in 1990, the credit union purchased the location and renovated it again in 1995. With its modern, spacious boardroom on the second floor, staff here consider this one of the best office buildings in St. Willibrord's branch system.

The branch today benefits from being in what DeBruyn describes as the wealthy Blenheim area because of the prosperous farms. "This is some of the best farmland in Canada and has some of the best farmers. They turn over a lot of cash." This relative wealth has also meant competition for St. Willibrord here. Although Blenheim has a population of less than 5,000, there are five full-service financial institutions in the area. "We have a lot of competition in the area, but I think it's healthy," says DeBruyn. "Over the last three or four years, the banks have really noticed we're competitors with them and that's really a good sign." While he knows that some people will never leave their banks because of loyalty, it also benefits St. Willibrord. "We have people who are loyal to us because they got their first loan from us."

Despite the competition, or maybe because of it, the Blenheim branch has been financially healthy through the 90s. As of May 2000, there were 2,515 owners, and Portfolio Totals of $85 million. Annual growth is among the highest of the branches, and while the agricultural sector provides the backbone of day-to-day business, "the commercial end in Blenheim has picked up," DeBruyn explains.

Modern-day farming in the Blenheim area

"The potential here is enormous. Small business has been attracted to the credit union because of our service levels."

DeBruyn and his staff pride themselves on their community involvement, and while the days of dropping by for socializing aren't quite the same as the early years, the friendly, social atmosphere still exists at the Blenheim branch. Throughout all the changes since the 1950s, St. Willibrord still maintains its small town feeling here and will strive to do so in future years. Says Cowan, "And I think that's the difference between the banks and the credit union."

STRATHROY

When fire devastated a portion of downtown Strathroy in early 1998, the Strathroy branch of St. Willibrord Community Credit Union was the first financial institution townspeople turned to for help in setting up a special relief account for victims of the fire. Branch manager Ken Peters believes it is only natural that people would turn to their community credit union in times of need. "We have been in Strathroy, in one form or another, since the credit union was started. People know us and trust us, and they see us as being affected by what happens to the community just as they are. We were happy to offer whatever help we could, including bridge financing for owners whose businesses were lost."

The attitude that the credit union is there to help members of the community has been central to its philosophy since late 1951 when Father Jan van Wezel conducted the first meeting, in a farmhouse near Strathroy, that led to the creation of the Strathroy/Watford division. Adrian Groot, Chris Van Loon, and John Strybosch were installed as the new division's advisory committee, with Strybosch as the cashier. During the first couple of years, weekly office hours were held at the Strybosch residence at 24 Saulsbury Street in Strathroy.

In addition to this office, several collection points were operated where deposits could be made, even though loan applications could not be accepted. Collection points were established in Watford, Arkona, Thedford, Grand Bend, and Parkhill, and by 1958, official office hours had been established in Watford and Grand Bend. John Strybosch travelled to these communities to accept deposits and complete loan applications. In Strathroy, the collection point was at the Catholic school, Our Lady Immaculate, beside All Saints Catholic Church.

ST. WILLIBRORD (LONDON) CREDIT UNION LTD.
Afdeling : S T R A T H R O Y.

Bestuur: P. van Engelen, R.R. # 2 Thedford, Voorzitter.
C. van Loon, R.R. # 4 Watford.
A. Groot, R.R. # 7 Strathroy.
J. Peters, R.R. # 3 Kerwood.
C. Smeekens, R.R. # 1 Thedford.
J. Michielsen, Box 474 Parkhill.
Kassier: J. Strijbosch, R.R. # 3 Kerwood. Tel: 26 R 13
Springbank .
Collectors: P. van Engelen, R.R. # 2 Thedford.
C. van Loon, R.R. # 4 Watford.
J. Michielsen, Parkhill.
Jo van den Berk, R.R.# 2 Grand Bend.

Aan de leden van de St. Willibrord Credit Union,afdeling Strathroy.

Geachte mede-lid,

Hiermede hebben wij het genoegen, U uit te nodigen tot het bijwonen van de jaarvergadering van onze afdeling, welke zal worden gehouden op WOENSDAG 25 FEBRUARI 1959 in de BOVENZAAL van het COMMUNITY CENTRE (ARENA) te
P A R K H I L L .

A G E N D A:

1. Opening van de vergadering door de voorzitter.
2. Voorlezing van de notulen der vorige algemene vergadering.
3. Jaarverslag en financieel overzicht.
4. Bestuursverkiezing : Aftredend Mr. P. van Engelen, Mr. C. van Loon en Mr. C. Smeekens, die herkiesbaar zijn. Uit de vergadering kunnen candidaten worden gesteld.
5. Koffie, sigaren. FILMVOORSTELLING.
6. Toespraak te houden door Mr. J. Boere, als lid van het Hoofdbestuur.
7. Mededelingen.
8. Toespraak te houden door de Geestelijk Adviseur.
9. Rondvraag.
10. Sluiting.

Namens het Bestuur van de Afdeling
Strathroy. P. van Engelen,Voorzitter.
J. Strijbosch, Secretaris.

Strathroy Annual Meeting Agenda, 1958

On November 1, 1964, the Wyoming and Strathroy/Watford divisions were amalgamated into the new Arkona division with John Strybosch as cashier. The new office was located in Arkona, becoming St. Willibrord's second office, after London, to offer full-time service to members. Weekly office hours remained in effect in Strathroy, Watford, and Grand Bend.

On May 1, 1974, a full-time office was opened in Strathroy at 80A Frank Street. The small office was at the top of a long, narrow flight of stairs on the second floor of the building. Initially, this operation was a sub-office of the Arkona branch where John Willemse was the cashier or branch manager. Martin Thuss was appointed office manager of the Frank Street location.

"Martin Thuss was one of the most well-respected and best-liked people around," says Ken Peters. "He was clearly the right person for the job at the time. He was a very honest man with great people skills, and the members really liked him. Very outgoing and involved in the church, he talked to everybody. He didn't spend much time in the office, but liked to go out and drum up business, and was very good at it. In large part due to his efforts, our reputation grew by word-of-mouth."

At the time, the membership was primarily, but not exclusively, Dutch/Flemish in origin. The bond of association was still the old Dutch/Flemish Catholic Diocese of London until the merger with Co-op Services whereby the credit union received a community bond for Middlesex. But according to Peters, even in the early days, people were not turned down because of their religion or cultural background.

Ken Peters started with the credit union while he was still a journalism student at The University of Western Ontario. "While I was at Western, John Willemse's brother was my room-mate. He happened to mention to me that they were looking for help in Arkona, so I took a summer job there, working the counter, and helping out at the Grand Bend sub-office from time to time. I would go up every Wednesday to look after the clients. I had not really planned on staying on, but I really liked the job a lot, so I stayed."

The office at 80A Frank Street was upstairs from a pizza parlour, and was long, narrow and small. "Initially, we were not very busy," recalls Peters. "I remember I would sit in the back doing paperwork, doing the posting by hand, for instance, because we didn't have machines then. Once in a while, a member would come in, and I would go to the front to help them, and then return to my work. We would have to close up at least once or twice a day to go and get

Dignitaries officially open office at 80 Frank Street, 1977. (l-r) *Chris Van Loon, Bob Eaton MPP, Martin Thuss, and Larry Condon MP*

cash, putting a little sign on the door saying, 'Back in ten minutes'. Then I would go and stand in line at the Bank of Commerce to get my thousand dollars so I could transact the credit union's business. We deposited our cheques there, then wrote a cheque from that account which was then sent to the Credit Union Central in Toronto."

Peters recalls how the money was handled in those early days: "Nowadays, eight thousand dollars won't last two minutes, but in those days, a thousand dollars would last all day. We only had a small floor safe. Anybody could have come in and robbed us at any time. We kept some money in a small wooden drawer, and the rest was in the safe which could easily have been lifted by anyone who really wanted it." Slowly, the business in Strathroy increased, and eventually the office was moved down to what had been the pizza parlour, a larger, more modern premises.

"Unfortunately, Martin Thuss was not with us for very long," says Peters. "He was quite ill, first with heart problems, and then cancer, and he was very rarely there after I started; we actually only worked together for a few weeks."

In 1977, Peters became the first branch manager of the new Strathroy branch office. "Before that, we were considered a sub-branch of Arkona, and as such didn't have a council of our own. So

I would meet with their manager, John Willemse, once a month, and attend their council meetings. Our annual meetings were also held over there, and our members would attend the meeting there." Jacqueline Baxter, who is now a financial service assistant in the Strathroy branch, also worked in the Frank Street office a day or two a week, starting in 1975. She came from the Arkona office to help out with the posting and record keeping.

While the office was located upstairs at 80A Frank Street, it had about 500 members. When the credit union branch moved downstairs in 1977, they had about $2 million in assets. "People were banking with us partly because John Strybosch had done such a terrific job promoting the concept of the credit union, and partly because of the positive influence of Martin Thuss." About the same time that the office moved downstairs, Erna Jansen was hired as the teller on a full-time basis.

Over the past 20 years, the branch has primarily served people in the agricultural and commercial community. "We understand the nature of their operations, and members like the fact that they get to deal with the same person year after year," says Peters. "Members don't have to deal with a constant change in account managers. The fact that we were small worked to our advantage. People didn't have to stand in line to get service when they came to us. Our rates were not necessarily better, but they were always competitive. It may also have been a little easier to get a loan from us at the time."

In 1994, the Strathroy office moved to its present location at 72 Front Street West. "At that point, we were the most profitable and fastest growing of the branches, and it was clear that we needed more space to serve our members. We also didn't own the building we were in on Frank Street, so something had to be done." The new building was erected on the site of what had been Derk's Auto Service.

As of May 2000, the office employed 18 full and part-time people, with 3,824 owners, and Portfolio Totals of $155 million.

According to Peters, some of the major changes the branch has seen since moving to the new location include an increased emphasis on the use of technology, and the sale of products. "Perhaps the biggest change over the past few years has been the addition of our financial planning services which we did not have four years ago. We now have a full-time financial planner on staff."

The drive-through service window has also been a major new innovation at the Strathroy branch. "The concept has met with real success. Members really appreciate the service." There is one lane with a machine that people can access, and another lane that goes to a window with a teller. "People like not having to get out of their vehicles, especially parents with small children, or on days with bad weather."

Peters believes that the nature of banking will change significantly over the next few years, but he also believes that St. Willibrord will still provide members with the option of having personalized service. "Some people prefer electronic banking, and we definitely cater to their wishes, but there are also those who want the option of speaking to an individual about their financial needs, even if it is just a basic deposit or withdrawal."

In July 2000, Peters celebrated the 25th anniversary of his career with St. Willibrord, representing almost the branch's entire history as a full-time office. Its success today is very much a result of his conscientious service.

As an essential part of the history of both Strathroy and St. Willibrord Community Credit Union, the Strathroy office will continue to be a vital component of the community it serves, and will continue to be a financial institution people can turn to in both good times and bad.

London East

The London East branch of St. Willibrord originated with the former Co-op Services London Credit Union. Co-op Services joined St. Willibrord by way of a purchase and sale agreement on October 1, 1977, but the building at 131 Wharncliffe Road South was not part of the transaction. It was assumed by the former Ontario Share and Deposit Insurance Corporation (OSDIC, now DICO) as part of their stabilization program. St. Willibrord leased the building for three years and then moved the branch to London East in 1980.

Wally Mutsaers had been with St. Willibrord, after a stint with the Royal Bank of Canada, since 1966, working first in the Kent and then the Albert Street offices. He was assigned the job of managing the former Co-op Services office which became the Wharncliffe Road Branch of St. Willibrord. "One of the reasons we leased the building for only three years was that the two existing offices on Albert Street and Wharncliffe Road were too close together. The intent was to relocate one of the offices to some other location in the city. Both credit unions had considered the east end of the city as a natural location for a branch office. St. Willibrord already had a fair number of members there, especially in the rural sector, and the former Co-op Services also had built up a substantial number of payroll deduction arrangements with companies and plants in this area, so the Dundas Street East location was considered ideal. We literally moved the entire branch operation to the new location, and closed the office on Wharncliffe. We moved here in December 1980, taking all the staff and all the accounts that were with us at the time."

There were two properties at the location when St. Willibrord purchased the land. One was a home and the other was a commercial building. Both were razed and an entirely new branch building was erected. This office underwent major renovations, including landscaping, and the creation of additional member parking, in April 1997. About half a million dollars were spent on the project. A portion of the second level of the building generates rental income as a dentist's office.

The move to the new location at 1867 Dundas Street proved a successful one, leading to growth in both memberships and services offered. Membership was made up, in large part, of a slightly different clientele than what people normally associated with St. Willibrord. There was still a large rural component in the membership of Dutch/Flemish background, but there was also a large number of business and consumer clients with a diverse cultural history.

"When I started 30 some years ago," recalls Mutsaers, "most people knew one another, not just from this country, but from back in the Netherlands. They knew the families and people's backgrounds and so forth. When we expanded with Co-op Services, we entered into a new phase in our relationship with the members. We were now dealing more with the general public than with a particular group of people. But even so, our membership had more of what I would call the cooperative spirit than perhaps they do today.

"Today's consumers are far more educated and more demanding than they were back then, and that applies not just to this organization, but to consumers in general. The impact of this new consumer awareness has been felt here as in all businesses. It means that we, as an organization, have to be on our toes and keep up our own knowledge and education. Our members today are selecting products because the rates are good or the product is good, not simply because they feel a sense of loyalty to the institution, or a sense of connection to the cultural community. As a result, they do not necessarily want to do all their business with St. Willibrord, but may take part of their banking needs to another institution. We need to prove to the membership that we can be competitive. We are now into second-generation consumers who are more aware of the kinds of financial services they want," adds Mutsaers. "There is still a strong element of the original membership, but they are not the majority any more. Even in rural branches, the makeup of the membership is changing because the farmers and the nature of the farming operations have changed."

Bringing in members from Co-op Services may have changed the nature of branch membership, but these changes were not felt immediately throughout the credit union as a whole. One of the more significant changes came in the nature of the loans the branch was arranging. "We started moving from agricultural and commercial loans more to consumer loans from the general public and regular wage earners," says Mutsaers. "That was something our credit committee had not been faced with much before. Many of the former Co-op members were consumers who lived paycheque to paycheque, whereas the people St. Willibrord had been dealing with before were immigrants who were trying to use loans to establish themselves. The object for the immigrants was not just to pay off a loan on one car, and then get a new car and a new loan. They were more interested in building equity than simply acquiring consumer goods."

By and large, St. Willibrord took the impact of these developments in stride. Not surprisingly, at the time of the merger, Co-op Services had a fairly large and regular membership turnover. A lot of the Co-op Services membership came from payroll deduction groups, and were often single people or people with two income families. They came primarily to St. Willibrord for convenience in paying back their loans. Then, when the loan was paid off, those members might move on to some other financial institution, or sometimes they relocated to a company that was not connected with the credit union.

The branch council was influenced subtly by the new membership. "When we took over from Co-op Services, we had a three member branch council," notes Mutsaers. "We expanded that to a five member council by bringing in two members from the former Board of Directors of Co-op Services. We had one council looking after both the Dundas Street and the Albert Street locations until each location got its own branch council in 1989." The function of all branch councils is to oversee the branch operations and be a liaison or representative of their membership, and the Dundas Street branch has always kept a balanced representation on its council between rural, self-employed people, and those who were more urban.

As far as the future of the branch and the credit union in general goes, it is Mutsaers' opinion that technology will have a major impact. "Technology will help bring about efficiencies, new services, and the kind of service delivery that will be required to fulfill consumer needs. In my time, we have moved from hand-posting and machine-posting to basic data systems, to an on-line system. And I am certain that this process of ongoing upgrading will continue." Mutsaers adds that today's technology will put products and services at the owners' fingertips. "These changes in technology will alter the nature of the relationship we have with some members. Some will see electronic services deliveries as wonderful. But there are others who will not want to make the change, either at all or too quickly. We will always be mindful of our responsibility to provide service to them in the way that makes them feel comfortable. The reality is, we don't actually need a physical location to service our members if they don't want to come in to the office. They can do their banking entirely through computers or over the telephone. But because this way of banking is not suitable to all our members, the bricks and mortar of St. Willibrord will always be here and needed."

This changing nature of the way St. Willibrord conducts financial transactions with its membership can be seen in the physical layout of the branch offices as they are either constructed or renovated. These new designs take into account the fact that fewer people will be coming in to see a teller, and more will be coming in for other financial services. This is why there is a reception area now, and why the people who deal with financial products have private offices which are more readily accessible to the members. The teller line is still here, but instead of eight wickets, for instance, there are now four. The number of tellers has decreased, yet the number of financial experts on staff has increased

And what about a cashless society? Can we anticipate a time when people will simply use cards for all their financial transactions? Mutsaers observes, "Since 1962, when I was still at the Royal Bank, people in the financial services business have always been talking about the coming of the cashless society. We are perhaps closer to that reality today, but it still isn't here. It is hard to imagine a time when people are not going to get information about their finances from another human being. People will still want to come in and talk to a financial adviser or a loans officer about what are, after all, major decisions."

To provide these new kinds of services and products, St. Willibrord will partner with other organizations to provide a broader slate of services. This will enable the organization and the branches to offer products to the owners without having to be restricted by its own financial assets. "This pioneering arrangement will in effect give us the ability to deliver virtually limitless financial products."

Wally Mutsaers had been the London East branch manager for almost its entire existence from the time of the Co-op Services merger in October 1977 until 1998. Jeff Segeren, who had already served in various positions within St. Willibrord, most recently as Watford branch manager, assumed the reigns in London East in May 1998.

Watford

The landscape leading into Watford is alternating stretches of rolling fields and flat farmland. Farms hug both sides of Highway 79 as paved and gravel roads stretch from it toward the horizon. On the main street of Watford sits the St. Willibrord branch office, a modern-looking building.

Agriculture plays a big part in this area of Southwestern Ontario, has been a key contributor to the credit union for many years, and continues to account for about 80 per cent of the business today. While the branch office has been a fixture on Watford's main street since a snowy day in January 1977, the Watford area has long been served by the credit union, from the days of Chris Van Loon operating a collection point in the early 1950s, to being handled from the Arkona office through much of the 1960s and 70s. Marian Rankin (née Van Loon), who worked in Arkona then, recalls coming here weekly when the livestock sales were on. "We would come to St. Peter Canisius Separate School here for two hours or more, with a cashbox."

But eventually, this demand created a need for some kind of credit union office for the village. When St. Willibrord saw that residents there were eager to have their own credit union, it decided to open up a branch building. Rankin, who was the first office supervisor, and Nancy Kremer, (née Van Gorp) the teller, were the only staff in those early days of 1977. As they look through a scrapbook with early photos of them in the office, which was smaller then, they remember with a laugh how slow business was. "It was very quiet," says Kremer. "We were by ourselves one at a time, with some overlap. It wasn't very busy. We'd sit and wait for people to come in, read the newspaper or a book." Starting out with a membership of about 345, the branch soon began growing and had almost doubled by 1980. Assets had almost quadrupled in that same period from $993,000 to more than $4 million. With the office open five days a week, transactions also became more regular. They handled just 320 in that first month after the opening but were doing more than 2,200 a month by 1979-80. "What we did in a month [back in 1977] we'd probably do in a day now," Kremer says.

As with most locations in St. Willibrord's branch network, members didn't just come in to do banking. Visits were a chance to socialize and share neighbourhood news. Although the branch is now a modern financial centre offering an array of services and products, that small town feeling and attention to service still persists. "Personally, I think we know almost 100 per cent of the people who walk through the door," Kremer explains.

Of course, there have been other changes since the late 1970s. Kremer recalls that when she left the credit union in 1979, there was no computerization in the branch whatsoever, but by the time she returned in 1987, the entire operation was completely automated. Membership growth at the Watford branch has been steady in recent years at about five per cent per year, while assets have been averaging

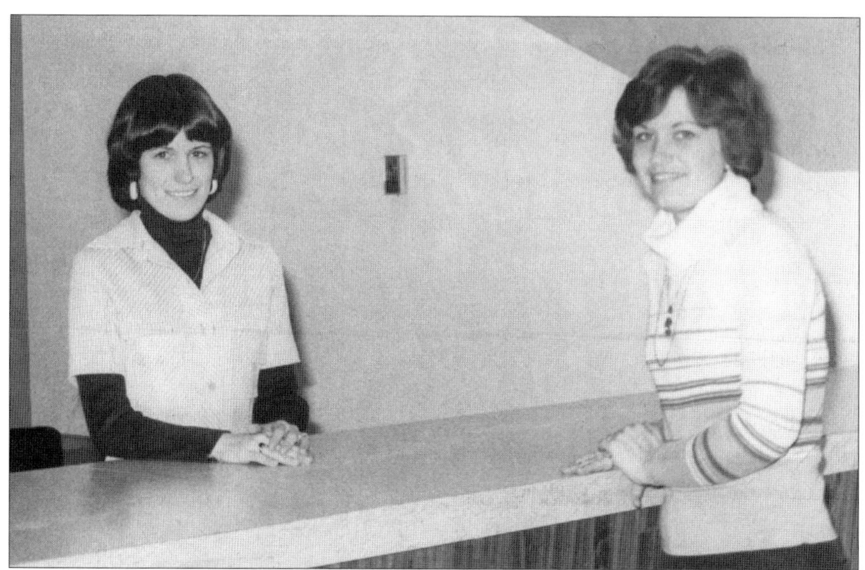

(l-r): *Nancy Kremer and Marian Rankin in 1977*

a 15 per cent increase annually for the past three or four years. Increases in membership usually happen because of word of mouth, although the Royal Bank's decision to close its Watford branch in 1994 did have some impact.

The Watford operation has also had success in building the commercial accounts side of its assets, with many Watford businesses becoming members of St. Willibrord. "Service is one issue," explains Jeff Segeren, Branch Manager until 1998. "Knowing people's names, doing things for them, going that extra mile."

Segeren, who has also worked at banks and is now at the London East branch, likes the freedom and time to develop relationships with credit union members. He says one of the differences was that, at the bank, "it was more a structured life. You came in and you started at a certain time and filled your day with a bunch of bank stuff. Here it's more flexible." Branches have the support of the credit union's administrative office but have enough autonomy to adapt to local needs.

A high point in the Watford branch's history was the renovations to the building in 1989 that gave staff and members more office space. During those messy renovations, members didn't seem to mind dealing with staff wearing jeans and less formal attire. The easygoing nature of this rural branch fit in nicely with that period of transformation.

What also works in the branch's favour is that most of the staff here have been in the community for many years, in some cases since their families immigrated to Canada. There are still a lot of owners with Dutch names, but the membership is changing as the credit union grows. The local branch council handles Watford members' concerns, but the work previously done by credit committees, such as determining loans, is now handled by administrative staff. That's a message that is still sometimes difficult to get across, says Segeren. "But one of the strengths of a small branch is that you know people very well."

As in other branches, the older members tend to be the ones who participate politically in the issues facing St. Willibrord, while the majority of members simply sees the credit union as a place that handles transactions. "For most people coming through the doors, the branch's financial performance is irrelevant compared to the service we provide," says Segeren.

Electronic and phone banking have helped the Watford branch spread its wings, geographically, with some members living long distances from the branch. That trend of not having to visit the branch in person will likely continue, but the friendly service within the building's walls will still keep people coming through the doors for years to come. In fact, although Watford is one of St. Willibrord's smaller branches, it handles many more transactions than some of the more urban locations and served 1,935 owners as of May 2000. "We all like our work," adds Rankin. "Because of that, we do our part and then some."

Jeff Segeren's established practice of offering professional, yet personal service continues under Branch Manager, Dave Vanos, who had been an account manager with St. Willibrord's Arkona branch, and moved to Watford in 1998.

London South

Karen Zeleznik is describing life at the London South branch. A woman had come in earlier to arrange a mortgage to buy her first house. She had been a long-time St. Willibrord member, and when all the necessary paperwork was signed, the woman gave the London South manager a hug.

"It is really wonderful to have this professional friendship with people you've dealt with all these years," Zeleznik says. "You take an interest in their first home and the ups and downs they have. That's nice."

"Professional friendship" is an ideal way to describe how the London South branch operates. It's about providing members with good service and high quality advice about financial matters, but it also means taking the time to get to know them, listening to their wants and needs, and building the kind of relationship that goes beyond dollars and cents. And while Zeleznik believes it's one of the strengths of her branch, she has a feeling it permeates the entire St. Willibrord organization.

"I don't know if it's the people we hire or just something we foster within the credit union, but the bottom line to any decision we make, and it's not corny, it's true, is how that is going to impact the member. It underlines every decision, every action we take. So if that's your focus, then the relationships obviously form from there."

She knows some new members at the branch are skeptical about this kind of service, but "it's not just black and white, dealing with financial statements," she says. "You actually get to know people." That knowledge builds trust, a key characteristic of the way London South operates. It is the trust, so apparent in the early days of St. Willibrord, that continues to this day.

As the second newest branch of St. Willibrord, London South hasn't had decades to build up its membership and get to know members like some other branches. But Zeleznik, who worked at London East for several years, had many members follow her to this branch when she took over as manager a few years back. The branch also got a boost when Northern Telecom closed and Penney Kerhoulas, who worked at the credit union there, joined St. Willibrord's staff and brought some members with her. There were, as of May 2000, 2,916 owners, and Portfolio Totals of $72 million, at London South. It's been a fast-growing area of the city for many years, but until 1990 when London South opened, St. Willibrord served that area of the city with its Downtown and East branches.

"London South was needed," Zeleznik explains. "It wasn't truly represented before then and there were a lot of people who were asking, 'When are you opening a branch in the south end?' They were willing to drive the distance to Downtown and London East, but people were waiting to be served in the area where they lived." The branch has averaged about 10 per cent growth in the past few years, which Zeleznik sees as a healthy pattern. "You don't want to go too fast; you want to manage your growth. As we get bigger, the challenges will be great to maintain that level of member service and retain our identity."

London South is very consumer-focused. Zeleznik believes the biggest challenge ahead in the 21st century is building the commercial side of the business, and to this end, a commercial account manager is now on staff. London South members tend to be savers rather than borrowers, but she'd like to see the branch manage more loans, mortgages and commercial accounts. Another challenge is continuing to make inroads in the southern part of the city. This branch is one of only two rented buildings in the organization and, for now, there is no plan to find a new home. While St. Willibrord has been around for half a century, there are still many people who aren't sure what the credit union is, she says. "People drive by and see our sign but they still may not be sure what it is. They see the name and they ask, 'Can I join? Do you have to be part of a union? Do you have to be Catholic? What's with this place?' So there's still marketing that needs to be done."

Those were questions even Zeleznik asked when she saw the London East branch being built in 1980. She didn't know how a credit union worked, or even why there were so many Dutch members, until she was hired and served as a part-time teller at that branch. Obviously though, she was impressed enough by how St. Willibrord served its members, because she's been with them ever since. "I can't imagine anywhere else where they give you the freedom to develop relationships."

That people-centred approach to banking is something Zeleznik likes her staff to take. And it may be one reason why the branch has won a Five Star Award for the past four years. This distinction enables St. Willibrord to recognize branches for excellence in sales, service, surroundings, strength and spirit. Branches are audited regularly by the administration to determine if customers are treated promptly, courteously, and professionally, among other measurements. "The bottom line is whatever is best for the member," she states. Her approach isn't the rah-rah chanting and cheering style some American companies promote, but staff here do like to have fun, socialize with each other after hours, and put a lot of stock in people skills. It's also why Zeleznik advocates giving constant positive reinforcement to her staff for work well done.

Communications with head office are open and honest. Branches set targets each year in conjunction with central administration, but she has freedom to set her own budget. The figures are reviewed to ensure they meet corporate goals, but "I don't feel pressure [to meet them]; I feel support." Zeleznik believes one of the best moves the company made was to create a position of branch operations VP so that information can flow more directly and easily between head office and the branches. There is also sharing among branches of new ideas and success stories, she says. Seminars that have proven successful in some branches can be packaged and applied at other branches too. Regular meetings with staff and with other administrators in the credit union also mean there's a free flow of ideas to ensure that things are being done the best way possible. "We're a team in this office, but what I'd like to see is the 10 branches be closer as a team. I think it can be done."

One of the changes she's seen, since starting to work at St. Willibrord, is a greater sales focus and an emphasis on branches becoming more proactive rather than reactive. "Ten years ago, when people came in and said they wanted a GIC, we gave them a GIC and then they left. Now, they get more than a GIC. They get advice, if they want it, and they get the time taken with them. We're doing that to give them value added, but we're also doing that to build the business."

London South members, she believes, are typical of the St. Willibrord makeup. They're working people putting money aside, building a good retirement portfolio, and looking for the kind of relationship you might not find at a bank. "And they're willing to drive here," Zeleznik says. Some members live as far away as St. Thomas and Port Stanley and are increasingly familiar with electronic and telephone banking to the point that they may actually only come into the building a few times a year. A few are active in the committees and annual meetings that St. Willibrord offers, but most are content as long as they're getting good service. "They just want to have somebody to talk to who knows their business and takes an interest in it. Someone who can give advice whether it be related to taxes or investments, and then they go on their way to enjoy life."

KITCHENER-WATERLOO

While St. Willibrord was in the throes of getting ready for the conversion to its new Ovation™ computer banking system, it was also completing a merger with the former Kingswood Industrial Community Credit Union in Kitchener-Waterloo. Kingswood had been operating for almost 50 years, first as a closed bond credit union serving the employees of Electrohome Ltd., and then, after 1990, as an open bond credit union serving the general public.

Kingswood had decided sometime in 1996 to conduct a comprehensive review of its long-term future. During 1997, it initiated a couple of meetings with other credit unions in the Waterloo area to see if there was any interest in a local group consolidation. Detecting no appetite from others for investigating such a step, and realizing it would not be able to provide full service to its members for the long term on its own, it asked for proposals from three credit unions, in January 1998, for potential merger conditions.

In March, the Kingswood Board selected St. Willibrord as the preferred candidate. They presented their plans to the Kingswood members as an information item at their March Annual General Meeting. After the usual due diligence process, the purchase and sale agreement was formally approved at a special General Meeting on June 25, 1998, and the transaction became effective June 30, 1998.

Aaron Bickell is branch manager of the renamed St. Willibrord Kitchener-Waterloo branch, moving to his new position there in May 1999 from his former position as Account Manager at the Stratford branch. He recalls that the change of management was a hectic time for all involved. "Jeanette Bell had been the manager here for some 30 years, and she had worked very long and hard to ensure the success of the credit union. But when it became clear that Kingswood would not be able to survive on its own, it looked around for a partner, and felt that St. Willibrord was the most viable with the best product line and the most compatible management style."

In spite of the compatibility of management styles, the five staff and about 1,400 members of the former Kingswood credit union had a lot of new procedures to get used to in a fairly short period of time following the merger. They had to become familiar with a different slate of products and a new way of doing things. Rose Klaehn, a service representative (teller) at the credit union since 1990, recalls that with the change in management came a new way of doing just about everything. "The process of changing from Kingswood to St. Willibrord went very quickly. There was a lot of new stuff to learn, but fortunately Jeanette [Bell] was there to help. After the merger, there were some mixed reactions from the members in response to the expanded slate of services. St. Willibrord offers a lot more than Kingswood ever could, and it was a little difficult for some people to know what services and products were best for them." In early April 1999, the Kitchener-Waterloo branch also adopted the Ovation™ computer banking system being used by St. Willibrord.

Once the merger was completed, Jeanette Bell retired, and she was clearly missed by her former staff. Bell had taken over the management of the Kingswood credit union from Elmer Fisher who had been instrumental in founding the credit union in the early 1950s. At that time, the credit union was known as the Electrohome Employees Kitchener Credit Union, serving only the Electrohome employees during that company's rise to power as a designer and manufacturer of electronics, primarily for the home entertainment industry.

From 1955 to 1969, Electrohome became a Canadian electronics success story, with sales figures of nearly $45 million, and over 2,250 people working in the 1.2 million square feet manufacturing space at the end of the 1960s. Following this period of rapid corporate expansion, Electrohome faced a flood of imported electronics, especially from Japan. Consequently, it had to cut its workforce in half and, for a time, the very survival of the company was in doubt. As the number of employees dwindled, so did the membership in the credit union, and in order to draw new members, the Electrohome Employees Kitchener Credit Union, changed its bond of association to allow people from outside Electrohome to join. At the same time, it changed its name to the Kingswood Industrial Community Credit Union, selecting that name from a number of suggestions that had been submitted by the membership.

Although Electrohome is still in operation today, it is functioning under reduced circumstances, and St. Willibrord currently rents office space in the factory. At the time of the merger, there were 1,400 members at the Kingswood branch. About a year after St. Willibrord joined with the Kingswood credit union, it merged with the much smaller B.F. Goodrich Credit Union, on May 31, 1999. This brought about 600 new members into the St. Willibrord family of owners. By May 2000, there were 2,300. As Aaron Bickell points out, the membership of the Kitchener-Waterloo branch of St. Willibrord has grown a great deal, and he is looking forward to moving to larger quarters.

With the opening of a new branch building in November 2000, residents in and around Kitchener-Waterloo will have the opportunity to experience St. Willibrord's continuing reinvention of banking first-hand. The K-W branch will be home to another St. Willibrord first – a Financial Education Centre. This centre will provide owners with innovative services such as financial health seminars, and Internet work-stations, creating a new dimension in credit union service delivery.

Located in North Waterloo, close to the Conestoga Expressway, the new branch location will be convenient for existing owners. The highly visible location was chosen because of its strong rate of residential development, thriving business sector, and close proximity to agricultural areas. Each of these factors will support St. Willibrord's growth strategy by making the branch accessible to a large number of potential owners.

Bickell is particularly interested in trying to appeal to members of the agricultural sector. "We would like to develop our agricultural membership, since we feel there is room for expansion here. As well, there are a lot of developing areas in Kitchener-Waterloo which currently have virtually no financial services. We see this as a real opportunity." As Bickell notes, the Mennonite Savings and Credit Union is very strong in the Kitchener-Waterloo region, but has a closed bond, and they have chosen to serve only those who belong to Mennonite, Amish, and Christian Brethren congregations. Waterloo Regional Credit Union has an open bond and is also influential. "We are not competing with other credit unions," he says. "We're competing with the banks."

NOTES FROM OUR STAFF

I have worked for other financial institutions and do feel that St. Willibrord stands out from the rest. St. Willibrord is a very friendly and concerned financial institution where you're not just a number.

When I joined this credit union almost six years ago as a staff member, I came to realize and recognize all the wonderful things St. Willibrord does for their owners.

We send welcoming notes to new owners, Birthday letters, Baby cards, Sympathy cards and donations. In general, there is a tremendous community involvement and St. Willibrord treats their owners as if they were family. I don't know of any other financial institution that truly does this.

Jenny Esselment

I have worked at St Willibrord for the past 18 years and have been impressed with the strong, open-minded but cautious leadership this credit union has. The financial services industry has gone through some huge changes over the past decade, and the credit union has adapted very well, keeping up to the changes we needed to make while ignoring some of the selfish changes the banks made to improve their bottom line.

There has been some solid business come to the credit union, not because we are aggressive and willing to take more risk than our competitors, but because common sense was used and not a thick policy manual. It is that approach that makes it enjoyable to do business with the credit union and to work here.

John DeBruyn

St. Willibrord is a great place to work! As a staff member, I am treated with dignity and respect, as well as appreciated. Our standards of excellence and owner service enable me to offer our members suitable solutions to the variety of problems they present.

Sharon Snow

After 17 years, I can say there has never been a dull moment at the Stratford branch. St. Willibrord is a very proactive organization, so that makes life very interesting with all our changes. It is a great place to work. They treat their employees very fairly.

It's the friendly, personal atmosphere that makes this credit union so successful. Seventeen years ago, John Strybosch believed in me, José Cozyn hired me, and I have been loving it here ever since.

Mary Jane Chambers

I feel strongly that St. Willibrord fits very well with my own personal value system – dealing with all kinds of people in an environment that promotes respect and dignity for all concerned.

My employer allows and encourages these relationships to develop for the mutual benefit of not only the owner and the credit union, but for myself personally. The support that is given by St. Willibrord to all its employees to grow and improve, in a satisfying environment, is always there and I couldn't imagine a more professional, yet friendly, environment in which to work.

Karen Zeleznik

I like working at St. Willibrord because of the interesting owners and staff I deal with every day. As well, there are always new things to learn. There is never a dull moment. St. Willibrord has a very friendly atmosphere.

Shirley Cook

What makes St. Willibrord an interesting place to work is its owners whom we get to know on a personal basis. They put their trust in us and we put our trust in them. Without our owners, we at St. Willibrord would have no job. Our success relies on our owners who deserve, expect, and receive our top quality service. But our owners aren't the only ones who make St. Willibrord an interesting place to work; it's

also our co-workers. Without their support and encouragement, work would be a very dull place. We work together, laugh together, and yes even cry together sometimes. We are always there for each other for moral support.

Marilyn Koot

I have had the opportunity to work in four different branches of St. Willibrord, and everyone was great to work with. They offer support, encouragement for personal growth, and are willing to go that extra mile. So many people get caught up in how much money they are making, they end up overlooking one very important fact – it's not worth it if you can't get along with the people you work with, or for.

St. Willibrord has a distinct "family feeling". You're not just another number here, but are a real part of a bigger picture.

It is great that as I progressed through the credit union, I had the opportunity on a few occasions to chat socially with our President & CEO and some of the VPs. I would guess that in many other big businesses, senior management is not as easily approached by other employees as they are at St. Willibrord.

Paul Arsenault

St. Willibrord has given me the opportunity to pursue a career in the financial services industry. I started as a front line teller in 1985. The credit union provided the opportunity and education for me to advance from one position to the next, from teller to Certified Financial Planner. I have learned this business from the ground up and am pleased that the credit union has assisted me in my career goals.

I truly believe that St. Willibrord cares about each owner and does its best to help/assist each one. The staff are given enough freedom in their jobs to really help the owner. The bottom line is important, but we are able to be profitable without forgetting who ultimately pays our way.

Wendy McLean

Roots &
Branches

CHAPTER 7

Breaking New Ground

On December 31, 1998, when most people were busy celebrating New Year's Eve with friends and family, several members of the staff at St. Willibrord Community Credit Union were gathered in the newly-renovated computer room in the basement of the Central Avenue building, anxiously watching a most important event in the credit union's history about to unfold. For the first time ever, St. Willibrord was to launch its own in-house computerized banking system, converting from the old, out-sourced system, to a new one run entirely by St. Willibrord. Failure of any major portion of the new system could have meant disaster for the organization and its owners.

Mary Jo Gale is a systems administrator at St. Willibrord who remembers vividly the "Conversion Weekend", and what life had been like for the harried people in the information systems division of the organization during the weeks and months leading up to New Year's Eve. "Before the conversion itself," she recalls, "we had a number of very late evenings, and even a few all-nighters, as we worked to get ready. But even after all our preparations and tests, the only way we could know for sure that everything would work was to actually launch the new program. I was in here [at the office] at 10 o'clock on Friday, January 1, to check on the success of the conversion, and I didn't go home until Sunday, January 3, at about 11 o'clock at night. People slept on cots, and even had rooms over at 137 Albert Street set up as temporary dormitories."

As Gale describes, staff had brought in sleeping bags, pillows, and changes of clothing, and they used the showers that were on the premises. Food was prepared by other staff who came in teams to cook. "It was nerve-wracking," Gale adds. "Fun in hindsight, but nerve-wracking at the time. We were certain we had planned for every contingency, and that everything would come off smoothly, but even so, we worried. In between periods of testing and bringing new systems on-line, people would find an empty office and sleep for a couple of hours. It was exhausting."

The offices of the credit union were closed January 1. For Saturday morning, January 2, they operated with partial service, and by Monday, January 4, 1999, the new system was up and running. St. Willibrord's new, entirely in-house, banking system was ready to usher in the new millennium.

It was the looming advent of the year 2000 that had made it imperative St. Willibrord make the switch to a new computer-banking system. As early as 1995, it had become apparent that the old system, which at that time was operated by the Cooperator's Data Services Limited (CDSL) out of Toronto, was going to have trouble dealing with calculations and formulae that involved the year 2000 and beyond – a problem which would eventually become known as the "Y2K bug".

Rick Hoevenaars recalls how the problem first showed up when the existing system was asked to do long-term calculations related to maturities on mortgages and term deposits that were going beyond the year 2000. "Although the problems we encountered at the time were relatively minor, it immediately became clear to us that we would have to find out exactly what the implications of the year 2000 would be for us." As Hoevenaars explains, everything in a computerized banking system is date-related and sensitive. If the dates used are incorrect, calculations will be off, resulting in incorrect account balances and debt calculations.

At this point, St. Willibrord, and other credit unions throughout the province, had to decide whether it was more cost-effective and secure to reinvest in the existing technology, or explore entirely new systems. "Credit Union Central of Ontario struck a committee," Hoevenaars recalls, "to request proposals for new systems for the 70 different credit unions that were using the old CDSL system." In addition, there were 20 other credit unions that were realizing they needed new systems as well. We put out a request for proposals, got a number of responses back, and narrowed the field to two, one from IBM and the other from CGI Group Inc., both of which had an in-house system which would give us our own banking system, the responsibility of running it, and a service bureau version (computer terminals linked to a mainframe) along the lines of what we had been using. We ultimately settled for the CGI in-house system called Ovation™." CGI was the authorized re-seller for Ovation™ under an agreement with Prologic Corporation, based in British Columbia, which had developed and still owns the software system.

The software and hardware needed to implement and operate the Ovation™ system cost St. Willibrord about $2.4 million. As well, some additional staff had to be hired to operate and maintain the Ovation™ system and be responsible for all the technical support. "The costs associated with the new system were considerable," notes Hoevenaars, "but they were ultimately less than if we had invested in the repair and upgrades of the old system."

Scott Ferguson, Information Systems Manager, adds that as far as the credit union was concerned, there didn't seem to be much point investing more resources in a system that was essentially old technology. "That system was already falling behind," he says, "especially in terms of being able to link in new technology such as PC banking, the St. Willibrord Call Centre, and the Internet. We were also concerned about putting money into a system over which we had very little control. It made more sense for us to own our own."

The conversion to Ovation™ was not without its challenges. "Not only did we have to learn how the program worked," says Gale, "we often had to redesign portions of the software ourselves to suit our needs." As the software was refined and installed, a testing area was set up on the top floor of 137 Albert Street, the former Children's Aid Society building now owned by St. Willibrord, adjacent to the back of the Central Avenue office. A team of close to 40 people from all levels of St. Willibrord worked exclusively to test aspects of the new program, working in close concert with representatives from Prologic, the firm responsible for the overall design of Ovation™. "People moved into London from out of town and lived in hotel and motel rooms for weeks at a time," recalls Gale, "doing testing and training at the testing centre."

The original deadline for the conversion to Ovation™ was October 31, 1998. But by the middle of September, it was clear to everybody that they were not going to be ready to make the changeover on time. "We had hardware still to be delivered, some of which had been back-ordered for weeks, and there were extra security features that it became apparent we would need. When you run your own computer-banking system, there are alarms and security systems which have to be installed." Even special doors to the new information systems offices were back-ordered.

Staff did not feel comfortable launching the system by the end of October, and it was decided to launch, instead, on New Year's Eve. "We wanted the switch done by the end of 1998. Then we would have a whole year to get comfortable with the operation before 2000." The system had been checked thoroughly with test dates up to 2005, so they were certain it was Y2K compatible.

The purchase and installation of Ovation™, with all the nail-biting tension of the New Year's Eve conversion was, in many ways, the culmination of more than twenty years of the gradual introduction of technology. St. Willibrord has been remarkably open to the uses of new technology, and has managed to be alert to changes in the world of emerging technologies that could benefit both the organization and the owners.

Prior to the advent of the first electronic devices, introduced to the organization in the early 1970s, all ledgers were done by hand. Helped only by rudimentary adding machines and typewriters, tellers updated passbooks by hand, kept the ledgers up-to-date by hand, and wrote their reports by hand. The IBM Selectric typewriter, with its correctable type, was a big step up the technological ladder from the standard Underwood typewriters that had been in the offices since the credit union's formation. Anyone who has ever had

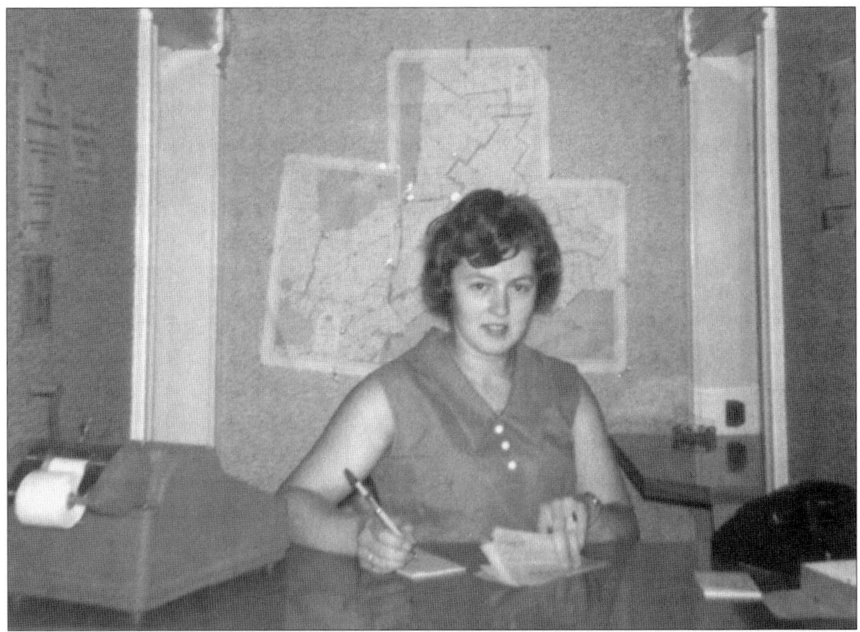

Wilma Bastiaansen beside a hand-cranked adding machine at the front counter, Arkona branch, 1965

the opportunity to work on an old Underwood, with its unwieldy keys and stiff platen, can appreciate how exciting the new Selectrics were. Hand-cranked adding machines could do basic mathematical functions, but they also gave their operators a considerable physical workout. Cash used by the tellers was recorded on paper, and the slips had to be continually sorted and balanced by hand.

It is interesting to note that two years before St.Willibrord invested in the first desktop computer, the organization had bought and installed what appears to be the first online Automated Teller Machine (ATM) in Southwestern Ontario. The ATM machines were initially seen by banking institutions as being little more than cash dispensing devices. The Bank of Nova Scotia had installed a machine in their Cherryhill (London) branch, but the machine was not "online", in the sense that it could not give the user immediate account balance information. The St. Willibrord machine was connected to the mainframe in Toronto and would give immediate account updates. People could use the machine to make deposits, withdraw cash, and transfer from one account to another.

Taylor Hamilton, year 2000 ATM user at Sarnia branch

This first machine lasted almost two decades, from its first installation in the spring of 1981, and was still in service until early 2000 in the London East branch of St. Willibrord. In terms of the evolution of technology, that machine qualifies as being an interesting relic of a distant past.

In 1971, the credit union purchased a Phillips mini-computer which, as Rick Hoevenaars recalls, was "about as big as my desk." The machine cost $50,000, a large sum of money in those days, and had only very basic computing abilities. "The machine had a slot, with a reader inside, into which we would drop cards bearing a small magnetic strip," remembers Hoevenaars. The strips stored member account balances.

Each member account was encoded on the magnetic strip, and as they were run through the computer, new transactions would be recorded. "It was part of my job to come in at month's end," says Hoevenaars, "and work from five until midnight, just running the cards through the computer." It was a matter of putting each card into the computer and letting the machine run through the calculations which the computer would then print out on a very large, and very noisy, line printer.

All the account and payroll information was maintained on that system, and even when the machine was taken out of service for member account maintenance, a gradual process from 1976 to 1980, it was kept to run the payroll system until 1983.

Member account maintenance was switched to a batch entry software system called Credit Union Banking Enterprise Two (CUBE II). It was operated by a company called CUData, first a joint venture between Cooperators Insurance and Credit Union Central of Ontario (CUCO), then by Cooperators alone as a subsidiary. The name of the company was changed to Cooperators Data Services Limited (CDSL). In 1976, small computer terminals were used in the branches to key in savings and

Staff training session in October 1980 on a CUData IBM 3600 Terminal
Above (l-r): *Mary Nicolai and Ann Westelaken*
Below, foreground: *Yvonne Brown (neé Haasen)*

chequing account transaction information that was uploaded to the mainframe system in Toronto through a 400-baud telephone modem with an acoustic coupler. The computer in Toronto would produce reports, which were sent back to London by courier every day of the working week. Between 1977 and 1978, loans and other account types were also converted to CUBE II. On October 27, 1980, St. Willibrord began to use CUData's online system, operated by CDSL.

In early 1982, St. Willibrord bought its first personal computer, an IBM PC. "The decision was driven by the fact that the PC used a spreadsheet program called Visicalc," says Hoevenaars, "and we saw it as a valuable tool for reporting." Hoevenaars recalls that there was no computer store in London that could supply the machine at the time, so he had to drive to a Computerland store in Waterloo, on a Saturday morning, to pick it up. "I had to use my brother's car," he adds, "because I was driving a Corvette at the time, and it didn't have room for the machine." St. Willibrord paid about $14,000 for that computer. The second personal computer was a Compaq "portable" about the size and weight of a sewing machine. As Mary Jo Gale recalls, the machine had a six-by-six inch orange-coloured screen and two 5¼ inch floppy drives with no hard drive.

The plan was that the ten people working in the London East branch would have shared access to the machine, and the intent was that people would start using it to write computerized reports. "But at first, people did not care much for it," Gale notes. "They were afraid to use the new computer, primarily for fear of breaking it. They knew it had been expensive, and were concerned it would be damaged if used incorrectly." The operators also suspected, not entirely without good cause, that they would not be able to access the information stored in the computer. "They didn't like the idea of not generating paper copy when they worked," says Gale, "and didn't trust the computer to store information correctly." So for the first six to eight months, people used the computer with some reluctance, at the same time as they created reports by hand. The effect was that the computer, supposed to help people work more efficiently and quickly, was in fact causing people to do all work twice.

Initial doubts surrounding the usefulness of desktop computers were eventually dispelled as similar systems were installed in all branches. "It became very exciting for people to be able to create reports, print them, and send them off in the courier bags," remembers Gale. By 1986, the administrative office had two computers, each one worth $8,000 to $10,000. The machines came with 30 meg hard drives. "We thought it was an unbelievable amount of [electronic] storage," says Gale. "We never thought we would ever use that much space."

As people grew comfortable with computers, it became clear that more computers would be needed, and that some system should be created that would allow the various computers to communicate with one another. "We had lineups at the two computer stations," says Gale. "Eventually, we had to create a booking schedule in order to give everybody access."

To meet the growing demand for the new technology, desktop computers were purchased for most of the staff at the administrative office, all connected through an electronic communications network called a Local Area Network (LAN). "We still weren't connected to anyone outside the organization," Gale adds, "but at least we were able to send information back and forth, in-house."

St. Willibrord had determined that technology would play an important part in its future, and went to considerable lengths to provide training for its staff, and finding ways of making people comfortable with the technology. An arrangement was made with consultants at Computer Associates in London to provide training and expertise for the creation of the LAN. Staff were allowed to take time off work to attend workshops on how to use the new spreadsheet and word processing software.

By 1992, LANs were introduced to each of the branches. By 1997, all the various branches were able to communicate electronically with each other, and with the main branch, in order to share files and e-mail. Again, this new technological development was viewed with some apprehension by those who had to operate it.

Tania Goodine, Sales and Marketing Manager, notes that, while management is able to track electronic customer transactions, the tracking is not used in an intrusive fashion. "Our sales support system focuses on the positive and encourages staff to offer information to owners about products they may need. But there are no consequences for the staff if a member declines." Mary Jo Gale adds it was perhaps not surprising there were some people who thought management could read e-mail being sent through the system. "We had to send a lot of memos to staff telling them that we could not read their e-mail. We worked very actively to build people's trust around the use of electronic communication because it allowed for better, more detailed communication, and cut down on the time we spent on the phone, leaving messages that might not be picked up."

In June 1995, staff such as Michelle Baker have desktop computers with wider capabilities

In late 1992, the venerable IBM 3600 and other "dumb" terminals were finally retired as direct, electronic banking systems were installed onto the desktop PCs. This development, perhaps more than any other, convinced people at St. Willibrord that they were getting their computer system together, and staff became a great deal more efficient. By then, just about all staff members had computers on their desks and could process transactions on the banking system, create correspondence, complete reports, access information outside the credit union, and communicate with each other. "At the same time," says Gale, "many of our computers were linked by modem to outside service providers, which meant that credit bureau reports could be easily obtained. We could also get our foreign exchange conversion rates on the computers every morning, and offer clearing of U.S. dollar accounts."

Along with the successful transition to the Ovation™ system in 1999, a year and a half earlier St. Willibrord had also inaugurated the Automated Contact Expert (ACE) contact management system. Designed by Dave Heron, Technical Analyst, and Chris Palmer, Senior Systems Analyst at the time, based on software requirement information provided by Stephen Bolton, Vice President of Branch Operations, and Tania Goodine, the ACE system is essentially a piece of software that lets staff representatives use a variety of smaller software applications. "Provided with a name and account number, ACE shows the user a complete profile of the owner, including his or her risk tolerance and investment objectives," says Goodine. "The representative can keep track of which products the customer purchases, how often, and it also helps to track staff sales performance. ACE makes things simpler for the staff, and it allows management to have a look at sales results." Because the software gives a staff member quick access to an owner's information, service can be much more personalized. ACE is also used to alert staff to campaigns that might be targeted to a certain group of the owners so that when someone comes into a branch or makes a call to the Call Centre, the staff will know that this person should be made aware of a particular product or service.

As Goodine points out, most Call Centre requests can be fulfilled by people in the Call Centre, but complicated financial planning and commercial requests are referred to a financial adviser or account manager. Whatever action they take on behalf of the owner is then summarized in ACE.

The need for a contact management system grew out of the opening of the Call Centre in June 1997. The Centre gave owners

Jennifer Campbell and Kathy Mendham in Call Centre

more than one avenue of access to St. Willibrord, which necessitated a consistent service for owners who might now be dealing with various people in the organization. The owner might talk to his/her financial planner, and then contact the Call Centre. It was felt that everybody who had contact with that owner should have access to the same information via computers.

This piece of technology changes the role of the tellers to make them far more sales/service focused. "Tellers are the primary contact with the credit union in most cases," adds Goodine, "although online and automated telephone services are changing that as well. Tellers are trained to spot particular financial needs and make referrals that will generate more business for St. Willibrord. They spend a good deal of time on product knowledge training, and sales training."

In fact, the role of tellers has changed to such a degree that they are now called "service representatives" to reflect their increased responsibilities. "Consequently, a number of people who now start as service representatives have the formal education needed to get into the financial planning field, and often move on in that direction within the organization."

In March 1999, St. Willibrord launched its Internet banking service for owners, a feature made possible by the conversion to Ovation™. As well, the popularity of the Internet had caused a number of owners to request computer access to their account information from their home computers. People wanted to be able to check account balances, transfer funds, and apply for loans, all through their home computers. As Goodine points out, the decision to create and then launch Internet service was, in large part, driven by owner wishes. "Before we launched the service, we predicted we would have about 500 subscribers within two months," recalls Goodine. "Yet within two days, we had 330. We have been especially amazed by the number of people who have gone to St.Willibrord's Web site and signed themselves up. This was not something we had expected."

According to Goodine, two months after the launch of the electronic service, nine per cent of the owners (2,700) had signed up for it. As of May 2000, 4,954 people subscribed to the service, (15.7% of owners). "Long before we launched the service, we were getting requests to provide online banking. We were perhaps not as quick to offer this service as some other financial institutions, and I think it is a testament to the loyalty of our owners that they waited, and did not switch financial institutions, while we were getting our own electronic services up and running." In addition, those people who don't have access to a computer can still do their banking by phoning 1-800-361-8222 from anywhere in North America.

Not surprisingly, one of the concerns expressed by many members using, or considering, electronic banking had to do with the security of their information. But as Chris Palmer points out, those fears have been unfounded. "The technology for security is not really new, but it works extremely well. There is really no way anyone can break in and have access to owner information."

That's not to say that people haven't tried. "There are odd attempts to access the computers from different parts of the world," he notes, "but the firewall protection is instructed to accept only certain kinds of information. Unusual activity can be tracked through the computer logs showing if someone has tried to make an unauthorized request, including where that request came from. But it is impossible to log on and just access information about owners' accounts."

If there is one technological innovation around which St. Willibrord's past and future seems to coalesce, it is the organization's Web site at www.mycu.com. The latest in electronic information dissemination and service provision attempts to create, in a "virtual" electronic format, that sense of community fundamental to the organization's creation 50 years ago. The web site extends the old credit union bond of association far beyond anything the founders could have imagined. Yet it does manage to draw people into the spirit, if not the actuality, of a community-based, owner-driven, financial institution.

Jackie Westelaken is Electronic Publishing Coordinator for St. Willibrord. One of her responsibilities is the creation and maintenance of the Web site as well as the company's Intranet, known as "Willynet". As Westelaken points out, the intent of www.mycu.com is to reach potential and current owners, and to communicate information about products and coming events. "Through the use of community images and informal text, visitors to the site are given a clear sense that the site and the credit union are theirs, and that they have a direct say in how things are done. There are more than 120 pages associated with the site and on every page, visitors have the opportunity to give us feedback or ask questions. And we respond to every question or comment."

In the months following the launch of the site in August 1998, it quickly became clear that this medium of communication was a popular one. With close to 10,000 visits a month, and a consistently

Andrew Tennant and Mary Jo Gale in the Operations Room

high satisfaction rate, people were taking every advantage of the Internet to communicate with, and learn about, their credit union. As of June 2000, there were 10,300 visitor sessions per month.

Several pages of the Web site are designed specifically for children, with activity pages and information about the Fat Cat® and HeadStart® accounts. There are also pages outlining the history of the credit union, and informing owners about the organizational structure and administration. By accessing this Web site, owners are able to gather a great deal of information about the organization.

"As the role of our Web site continues to develop, we will add the capability of automatically informing owners about coming financial seminars," adds Westelaken, "and we will also add an e-mail database which will allow us to send information to owners." The Web site continues to be a viable information channel and service option, becoming an increasingly sophisticated educational, marketing, and two-way communications tool.

In addition, Goodine points out that as the Web site grows, the Call Centre will become more integrated into the site, allowing users to access Call Centre help through the push of an on-screen button.

"There may even be a camera component, eventually, for those who would like face-to-face communication. And theoretically, we may be able to use the cameras for retinal scans for identification, which would eliminate the need for documents to be signed." Before long, Goodine predicts, there will be a large number of people who will do all their credit union business from a distance without setting foot in a St. Willibrord branch.

Clearly, the creation of www.mycu.com was a success and, as Goodine points out, compared with the creation of a new branch, the associated costs were negligible. "The use of this kind of technology does not really change our traditional beliefs or sense of ourselves as being community-based and focused," Goodine notes, "If anything, it enhances our ability to provide those services to a much larger audience than a branch, and it allows us to maintain our position in the financial community. But there will always be a place for those who want to walk into one of our branches to conduct their business."

In spite of the remarkable technological changes in the way the credit union conducts business, it has managed to maintain a focus on the importance of good owner relations. Without losing sight of the fact that its owners ultimately determine what their relationship with St. Willibrord will be like, the organization has managed to develop and implement the technology which allows the credit union to deliver services that keep it a competitive, attractive alternative to traditional financial institutions.

A Culture of Consensus

Developing a shared vision which energizes an organization, while serving the needs of many owners and stakeholders, has been an ongoing challenge for St. Willibrord Community Credit Union. Yet from the beginning, people involved at the grass roots worked with others to promote the mutual benefits of a credit union, create an organizational framework which would meet its needs, and encourage the development of staff who appreciate its principles. A responsible but proactive relationship with government, the media, and the community at large, has also been part of the continuing process.

As any organization grows, it must create some type of administrative structure. All positions in the formative days of St. Willibrord were voluntary, but as the credit union grew and more people became paid employees, a new system was needed which was clear, flexible, and capable of dealing with inevitable changes.

In his book, *The New Realities*, management guru Peter Drucker makes the following observation about the creation of the corporate, hierarchical management model: "At that time (the 1870s, the dawn of the emergence of the concept of 'business management'), the only large, permanent organization around was the army. Not surprisingly, therefore... the command model, with a very few at the top giving orders and a great many at the bottom obeying them, remained the norm for nearly one hundred years."

As Drucker and others have gone on to note, this military-style management model has undergone a number of changes in the past 30 years, but in spite of efforts to flatten organizational structures and involve employees in the decision-making process, most organizations, and especially more conservative ones such as financial institutions, still operate with a hierarchical administrative structure with the chief executive officer supported by a small group of senior managers at the top, and the people in the entry-level positions at the bottom.

St. Willibrord Community Credit Union uses some of this traditional organizational method, but with a significant difference: rather than being at the top of the structure, the office of the President and Chief Executive Officer, currently occupied by Jack Smit, sits in the middle. The chain of command and communication follows a conventional format from entry-level positions up through supervisors, managers, and vice presidents to the president and CEO. The president reports to the Board of Directors, which is accountable to the delegates who, in turn, are elected by the owners at large. The effect has been to create an administrative structure at St. Willibrord that is hourglass-shaped rather than the customary pyramid, with the owners on top, whose voices are heard through their elected delegates.

"I report to the Board," says Smit, "to keep them abreast of what I am doing and how the organization is functioning. It is vital that they have a clear understanding of why things are done and how things work." Smit notes that his role is to act as a coordinating agent between the administration and the staff of St. Willibrord, and the Board and the owners. "One of my primary responsibilities is to create an environment where the staff is treated right and have opportunities for development. If I do my job well, staff satisfaction will translate into excellence in service to our owners."

Tony Strybosch, a brother of John Strybosch, is Chair of the Board of Directors, as of May 2000, and has been since 1998. He observes that there have been a couple of significant changes in the way the Board interacts with the administration of St. Willibrord. "When I first became a member of the Board," he recalls, "it met monthly with what was then called the general manager. When Jack took over, he very quickly introduced the practice of bringing all senior managers into the monthly meeting." The change in practice meant that six senior managers met monthly with the nine Directors, a situation which Strybosch recalls made some of the Directors feel a little intimidated at first. "But it soon became clear that the new format gave balance to the decision-making process, decisions made based on information provided primarily by senior management balanced against the collective experience of the Board." All major decisions affecting the credit union are discussed between senior management and the Board of Directors.

It is rare that there are significant differences between the desires of senior management and the Board. Goals of the organization are shared and subscribed to by both groups, and both groups have the success of the credit union as their central interest. "There can be differences between the desires of an individual owner and the collective ownership," notes Smit. "When that happens, the interests of the collective have to take precedence. We have to provide competitive service and pricing, and at the same time ensure that the organization is viable; we have to be efficient in what we do to maximize benefits for the owners."

On the administrative side, the president and CEO hires the senior management team, which consists of five vice presidents. The vice presidents are organized by area of function, for example human resources or owner relations. With the senior management, other specialist managers in administration, and the ten branch managers, St. Willibrord has a complete management team of 23 people. The other staff reports in one way or another to this team.

The way decisions are made depends a lot on what kind of decision is needed. If it is a matter of creating and issuing a new class of shares, that ultimately has to be approved by the owners. The decision-making path would involve determining what elements have to be approved and by whom. In this particular case, it would require both a change to the Articles of Incorporation and a subsequent formal offering of the new type of shares. A significant decision of this type would be extensively researched by management, then recommended to the Board who would, in turn, consult with the branch councillors and delegates before formally presenting it at the Annual General Meeting. This process might take a few months. The more important the decision, the longer it takes to reach a resolution. Some decisions, of course, can be handled quite quickly. After the Board has approved in principle, or has asked for more information, the action can be implemented. Above all, both the Board and the senior management team feel it is vitally important the Board should never find itself in the position of trying, or needing, to micro-manage the organization. "I have seen that happen with other corporations," says Smit, "and it invariably ends in disaster."

If the administration of St. Willibrord ever contemplated entering into a contract, the value of which exceeded 15 per cent of the company's assets, that decision would automatically be sent to an annual meeting for a decision. The purchase of another credit union would be a case in point, provided the investment was over 15 per cent of assets. The purchase of the former Kingswood Industrial Community Credit Union in 1998, for instance, was under the 15 per cent limit. The Board had the authority to make that decision on its own, but the administration reported these activities to the owners, months ahead, through councillors and delegates, so if they had a concern or objection, the Board would have heard about it well in advance. The Board members could ignore these concerns if they chose, but would do so at their peril because they hold elected positions.

Since 1997, following the 1996 rewriting of the St. Willibrord Community Credit Union bylaws, and according to the new Act governing credit unions, there has been remuneration associated with being an elected representative. As of May 2000, branch councillors get $50 per meeting they attend, while directors receive $100 for a full Board meeting and $50 for a committee meeting; the Board Chair gets $150 for a full Board meeting. If a director is a delegate to the Credit Union Central annual meeting, he/she gets $100 a day for every full day, plus all expenses. The amount of money involved with being an elected representative does help to offset any costs associated with holding the positions. Some meetings are held during working days, for instance, and the remuneration helps to compensate for any lost wages or vacation time.

Before 1997, elected positions were all voluntary, and not everyone at St. Willibrord was at first happy with the change to financial compensation. But as Harry Joosten notes, "If you want to attract younger people, especially those who have children, and avoid the tangle of paying people with children but not paying those without, which would be discriminatory, we thought that to defray any indirect expenses associated with these positions, the credit union should initiate a remuneration program." Delegates still serve on a voluntary basis. In fact, as Tony Strybosch points out, the majority of elected positions are still voluntary, without remuneration.

St. Willibrord, with its branch councillor and delegate system, has never had trouble finding people interested in serving as director, although, traditionally, the position was filled by acclamation. However, in January 1999, six people stood for election for three positions, and the next year there were four candidates for three positions.

THE EMERITUS CLUB

Membership in the Emeritus Club at St. Willibrord Community Credit Union is made up of people who have served for nine years or more as a Branch Councillor, Director, or as a member of the former Credit or Supervisory Committees.

As well, members of this club are persons who retired from St. Willibrord while in a management position.

Emeritus Club Members receive the monthly Gazette newsletter, invitations to the Annual General Meeting, and the Elected Representative Appreciation Day held in June each year. As of June 8, 2000, the club had the following members:

Alastair Brent	John Roks
Maria Bruijns	Gerald Sanders
John Cowan	Case Smeekens
José Cozyn	John Strybosch
John De Groot	Herman Van Bakel
Tony De Groot	Don Van Goozen
Bart De Vries	Betty Van Haren
John Féron	Chris Van Loon
Harry Giesen	John Van Noort
Bill Intven	John Van Werde
Dan MacDonald	Bill Van Westerop
Tony Marsman	Arnold Vander Helm
Wally Mutsaers	Diane Vandervelden
Arnold Nooyen	Arnold Vandewiel
Henry Olsthoorn	Harry Wijsman
John Peters	John Willemse
Gus Roelands	Henry Wydeven

Some owners are recruited for elected positions by candidate recruitment committees, whose job it is to stimulate nominations. Those owners proceed through the usual nomination process and when owners see the names on the ballot, they are not able to tell who was approached by the recruitment committee, or who put themselves forward on their own initiative. That way, the owners will elect a candidate based on his or her abilities, not because of committee suggestions.

Prior to 1990, what was then called the Nominating Committee would put forward its candidates of choice for the available positions. At the annual meeting, members would know that certain candidates had been especially put forward by the Nominating

Committee. The floor would be open to further nominations, but the underlying message was, of course, that the committee had already indicated whom they felt should be elected. Very few sought nominations from the floor, but there were instances of such candidates being successfully elected.

Over the years, the Board has experienced remarkably little conflict. The St. Willibrord system provides a way for directors to retire, whether on their own initiative or not, and to do so with their reputation and dignity intact. Regardless of director, councillor, or delegate position, if an incumbent whose term is expiring has not been living up to his or her responsibilities, the recruitment committee will simply remain silent with respect to the person in question and the nomination. As the advance nomination period progresses, the individual does not get a supporting call from the recruitment committee. The person can still submit a nomination however, but the message that the time to retire has come will be clear. It can then be announced that business or family pressures or whatever, are forcing him or her to step down, and everybody's feelings are spared and respected.

A balance of power between the Board and the senior management team is achieved through a shared vision of what St. Willibrord should be. "I am a long-term thinker," says Smit, "and fortunately, the Board is as well." The strategy, notes Smit, is not to invest so much in the future that there are no resources left to generate returns in the present. "There was some opposition to the purchase of Co-op Services because some people felt too much was invested in something that wouldn't have returns for many years. The purchase of the former Kingswood credit union falls into the same category." But, as Smit emphasizes, if the credit union does not make these kinds of long-term investments, it puts itself in danger of stagnating. As the St. Willibrord vision statement says, "We will be Southwestern Ontario's preferred source for quality financial service", and will achieve this goal through the continuing cooperation between Board and senior management, and through cautious growth. St. Willibrord normally wants to generate 10 per cent growth in assets annually. "To achieve that," says Smit, "we have to watch our growth, and our staff complement."

Along with an annual growth target of 10 per cent, St. Willibrord also remains open to mergers with other credit unions. As Tony Strybosch observes, cooperative financial institutions currently comprise about 7 per cent of the financial institutions in the province. "We think it is important for people to have a real choice when it comes to selecting a financial institution," he says. "I think that should be closer to 50 per cent, in order to provide a better balance of options for society." But as Jack Smit and other members of senior management point out, those mergers will come slowly and only with careful planning.

One of the interesting aspects of the structure at St. Willibrord is that the owners are, at the same time, customers and voting owners. They have a keen, vested interest in the success and operation of their credit union, and are truly stakeholders.

As customers, owners want quality, service, a fair price, and respect. Those owners who are Class B Investment shareholders are concerned with the financial well-being of the credit union. They want to know that their investments are safe and generating a reasonable return. "As managers, we have to keep that duality in mind," says Joosten. "There are things we could do to increase shareholder satisfaction, but it would be at a potential cost to customer satisfaction. As voters, they want an open, honest communication within a fair, democratic system of electing representatives and making decisions."

The other major stakeholder group is the staff. Some of their interests will sometimes compete with those of the owners. If the staff wants a considerable increase in salary, that could slightly decrease the net financial performance of the credit union. If they want more training, that comes at a cost as well. The challenge to management is to ensure all stakeholders are heard, their concerns are acted upon, they are all treated with respect, and that the interests of one group are not put above the interests of another.

To be sure, St. Willibrord is, and has always been, a strong supporter of the life-long learning process. Theresa Mikula, Vice President of Human Resources since 1992, points out that the organization offers a variety of development courses to staff. "Some of the courses are compulsory, since they emphasize skills they need to do their jobs and advance within the organization. Other courses are optional, and are designed for staff who have certain career track or personal development aspirations. That way, long before a position becomes open, they can work to make themselves the best candidate for the position." In addition, the credit union will help staff with educational upgrading, paying for the course and any related learning materials, provided that the staff member receives a passing grade.

Staff have annual performance reviews based on monthly,

individual, checkpoint sessions so that people can see how they are performing on a regular basis. How they perform affects their salary since there is a merit pay component. Remuneration for each job is on a scale and, based on performance, employees can move up to full pay. On occasion, people who are simply not a good fit for the organization have been let go. However, the credit union is very good about assisting people who have gone through difficult times, whether emotional or physical, and there is a confidential employee support program. The organization goes to considerable lengths to maintain staff loyalty.

While St. Willibrord management has an open-door policy with respect to making themselves available to the staff, the preferred line of communication is through the accepted hierarchy. "When John [Strybosch] was here, we had a totally open office," recalls Smit. "His desk was out in the open, and anybody could come and talk to him about anything at any time. This may have been a good way to stay in touch with a relatively small staff, but there was no privacy whatsoever, and that was a problem when people had to deal with confidential matters. In addition, as the number of staff increased, I believe efficiency was affected simply because of crowding. Everybody could always hear what everybody else was saying."

As the staff complement grew, official lines of communication were established. The staff also communicates in branch staff meetings which happen at least monthly, and sometimes more often. Staff members are encouraged to take a problem to their supervisor, who will then take it to the manager if need be, and so on up the line. "But if there is problem of a personal nature, or there is some other reason why a staff member is not comfortable going to a supervisor, he or she can certainly come to me or any one of senior management."

There are a number of external stakeholders as well. Other credit unions have a stake in the performance of St. Willibrord because how it performs reflects on them as part of the collective credit union image. The government and the regulators have a stake in the enterprise as a secure, reliable, financial institution. St. Willibrord also needs to be concerned about the credit union's suppliers and partners. "If we grow," says Joosten, "it means more business for them and if we fail, they lose a major customer. If we are fair with them, we have a good working relationship. If we are not upfront with them, it may cost them money, and their attitude towards us will change."

ST. WILLIBRORD SUPPORTS AND CONTRIBUTES

From 1996 to May 2000, these are a few of the organizations that St. Willibrord has supported through donations, contributions or investments of $1,000 or more.

Children's Hospital of Western Ontario

London International Children's Festival

Women's Community House

Covent Garden Market, London *(A founding partner)*

Ridgetown College/University of Guelph

University of Western Ontario *(Scholarship endowment)*

Orchestra London *(Elementary school outreach)*

Waterloo-Wellington SEED Community Loan Fund *(Entrepreneurial micro-lending program)*

In addition to monetary donations, St. Willibrord staff donates time and expertise to various local initiatives such as youth sports, and youth education, in both elementary and secondary schools.

Finally, there is the general public who are also viewed as stakeholders in the sense that they will be concerned about things such as how well the organization keeps up its properties, whether or not St. Willibrord is a good employer, pays its taxes, and gives back to the community in the form of helping charitable organizations.

Because one of the key corporate values of St. Willibrord is openness, there are a number of ways the organization communicates with all stakeholders. It communicates primarily through the Board, but there are also a number of newsletters and monthly branch council meetings where a set of reports reflects each branch's performance. Annual owner satisfaction survey results are posted in these reports. The strategic business plan is also made available to all staff and elected representatives.

The various owner information meetings are well attended. On average, about three per cent of the owners attend the branch annual meetings. The smaller, rural branches may get up to five or six per cent. These are actually good percentages when one considers that if there is a credit union membership of more than 30,000, 10 per cent would represent 3,000 people, and large meetings may mean that people will feel less able to participate in the process. Some local meetings are attracting around 125 people, and that's large for a town-hall meeting.

The difficulty with a philosophy of open communication with all stakeholders is that there may be some details the organization would like to keep in-house. As Joosten notes, "There is some information about our planning which I would prefer other financial institutions were not privy to. Once you distribute information to 129 elected representatives, almost 200 staff, and 34 Emeritus Club members, there are no longer any secrets. But we do trust that our stakeholders will keep the interests of the credit union uppermost in their minds."

St. Willibrord definitely wants the mass media to feel that this credit union is a reliable source for accurate information about credit unions in particular, community-related credit union activities, and the financial services industry in general. That intention also extends to the municipal, provincial, and federal governments, whose representatives may be looking for information related to financial services. "We certainly make sure that we are available to both the media and the government," says Joosten.

There are three people at St. Willibrord who can talk to the media on their own accord: the Chair of the Board of Directors, the president and CEO, and vice president owner relations and corporate secretary. Harry Joosten is serving in this latter role at present and notes, "By and large, relations with the media are very good. We try to make ourselves available to them, and they, in turn, try to get the story right. Over the years, there have been very few instances where I have had to actually call the media following a story to correct some piece of information.

"Our marketing agency, Connections Integrated Communications, does help us a little in the area of corporate writing and media releases, but it is important for us to speak with one voice to have our message be consistent. Credit Union Central of Ontario will sometimes help on a larger credit union story."

CUCO and Credit Union Central of Canada (CUCC) supply all the credit unions with information about developments at the governmental levels. A case in point occurred when the Ontario Legislature was working on the new Credit Unions and Caisses Populaires Act. The credit unions and caisses populaires in Ontario formed a coalition so they could present a common front to the government, supported by a letter-writing campaign to help move the legislation through quickly. As Joosten notes, the public relations

St. Willibrord welcomes new credit union rules

Free Press staff

A local credit union welcomed new rules designed to help them expand nationally to offer greater alternatives to the big banks.

"We still have a vision of a national services entity," said Jack Smit, president and chief executive of London-based St. Willibrord Community Credit Union and vice-chairperson of Credit Union Central of Canada.

Regional credit unions have long discussed pooling their resources to provide e-commerce, wealth management and small and medium-sized business services, Smit said.

"What the government is doing here, they're saying they'll accommodate that initiative for us."

The new legislation also begins to bridge the gap between how Ottawa oversees the banking system and how provinces regulate credit unions, said Harry Joosten, St. Willibrord vice-president for owner relations.

"There should be increased harmonization between federal and provincial regulations," Joosten said.

"This is looking to be a step down the road. It's the first time where it's formally put forward as legislation."

Banking legislation highlights

- Defines a review process for future bank merger proposals, involving Parliament, public and federal regulators.
- More flexible ownership rules for chartered banks aimed at letting them grow to compete against heavyweights in the global industry.
- Changes to the rules governing credit unions designed to help them expand nationally to offer greater alternatives to the big banks.
- Proposed financial consumer protection bureau.
- An independent consumer ombudsman.
- Asks banks to provide all consumers with access to a basic low-cost account.
- Individual shareholders can own 20 per cent of voting shares of major banks, up from current 10-per-cent limit.
- But those banks must still keep Canadian headquarters and their boards three-quarters Canadian.
- Smaller banks with $1 billion to $5 billion in assets — including Quebec-based National and Laurentian banks — allowed to have controlling shareholders.
- Banks may set up a holding structure, which could then have separately regulated subsidiaries including retail banks, credit card companies, insurance firms.
- Life insurance companies, securities dealers will have access to the payments system.

Canadian Press

The London Free Press *article reflects media consultation with St. Willibrord, June 14, 2000 (Reprinted with permission)* work is paying off. "Because of our efforts, our relationship with governments at all levels is good, and we work to keep it that way."

The regulatory relationship between St. Willibrord and all other Ontario credit unions and the provincial government arises from an act called The Credit Unions and Caisses Populaires Act which is administered by the Financial Services Commission of Ontario (FSCO), an agency of the Ontario Ministry of Finance. When the credit union started, it was governed under an act administered by the Department of Agriculture, then by Consumer and Commercial Affairs and, in 1994, the act became the responsibility of the Ministry of Finance. An updated act governing credit unions was proclaimed on March 1, 1995. This wholesale rewriting of the old Act was the first review of its kind since 1976.

The Deposit Insurance Corporation of Ontario (DICO), a Crown agency, is in charge of deposit insurance, and also has some regulatory powers because, if they are to insure deposits, they have to ensure that loans are safe. In the past, there has been a separate set of reporting required for the two agencies, but in the fall of 1999, the FSCO and the DICO started to work together to develop a common set of report data from which each agency will take information required.

Although St. Willibrord has always managed to operate within the regulations, there has been one bone of contention which has dogged the organization just about since its inception, and that has to do with the lending limits. St. Willibrord has always been somewhat constrained by the allowable loan amounts, a natural tension between wanting to fulfill the needs and wants of borrowers and staying within parameters that the government thought prudent. Part of the trouble was that the government of the time, especially in the early days of St. Willibrord, was not used to dealing with credit unions that catered to the self-employed commercial area, and the government officials were not willing to give the go-ahead.

But with the revised credit union Act, a new set of regulations was developed that took into account the lending licence rather than the credit union's lending bylaws. Prior to 1995, every single bylaw had to be approved by the Ministry for it to become effective. Now, only certain substantial or prudential bylaws must have approval from the Ministry through the Financial Services Commission of Ontario. Other than that, the credit union can organize its own affairs however it sees fit, so if the Board wants to change a bylaw, it may do that, provided it is within the regulations, and doesn't involve a change in the loan licence. If the credit union wants to increase the loan limits, it still has to apply to the Ministry. St. Willibrord does have a syndicated loan licence which allows it to get a partner if it wants to make a very large loan.

Along with its own internal auditing systems, St. Willibrord is audited annually by the independent accounting firm of Ernst & Young. As well, every 18 months, St. Willibrord is inspected by DICO, sharing the results with FSCO.

While fulfilling obligations to certain government regulations, overseeing internal and external audits, and responding to a rigorous system of inspections, St. Willibrord has dedicated a significant amount of time and energy in order to keep abreast of changes in the modern business environment. One key part of this strategy is a comprehensive review of its business processes and corporate vision.

Under the guidance of a senior management steering committee, and headed by Diana Jordan, Business Process Review Administrator, 12 sub-committees within the organization have been evaluating St. Willibrord's various business processes, forms, and procedures with the intent of improving service, making the corporation more streamlined and efficient, reducing redundancies, and taking full advantage of the Ovation™ banking system. The review process began in April 1999 and is scheduled for completion in September 2000.

At the same time, the various stakeholders of St. Willibrord were given the opportunity to express their opinions about the direction they felt the credit union should be taking through a process known as "Picture Tomorrow". By bringing together a variety of focus groups, the organization hopes to learn where the credit union should be concentrating its efforts in the coming years. As Jack Smit points out, the "Picture Tomorrow" evaluation process is intended to provide senior management with some insights into what changes the various stakeholders believe the credit union should consider. "It is difficult for any of us to say where we are going to be 10 years from now. We can adapt to change, I am confident of that, but exactly what those changes will be is uncertain. That is where the 'Picture Tomorrow' process will be helpful."

One area where St. Willibrord plans to make some changes in the next few years is in the area of community involvement. "Being involved in the community is not only good for our business through the connections we will make," notes Jack Smit, "but it will also be good for the community through the contributions the credit union can make in terms of both financial and human resources."

Don Duffield and Brenda Clark of Arkona branch at Children's Hospital Fundraiser, September 1999

Albert Street branch staff and council Spring car wash and bake sale to support Children's Miracle Network Telethon

To a New World

CHAPTER 9

In the main ballroom of the London Convention Centre, lights are dimmed and a large screen in the right front corner of the room is filled with charts and statistics. A computer-generated PowerPoint™ program provides images on screen, detailing the previous year for St. Willibrord Community Credit Union. Some 150 delegates and observers have already been meeting in this room, on a cold January morning, for a couple of hours.

They have heard good news about the credit union's previous year. The number of St. Willibrord owners has increased six and one-half per cent over the previous year to bring the total to more than 31,000, making it the 21st largest credit union in Canada. There was a successful launch of online banking, deposits increased by eight per cent, and total assets grew to more than $459 million. Expansion to the Kitchener-Waterloo area one year earlier led to the BFG Employees Credit Union joining forces with St. Willibrord's newest branch. It was, indeed, one of the credit union's most profitable years.

The branch councillors, delegates, and other owners sit at long tables set up throughout the room and watch as the credit union's Board of Directors and senior staff, at the front, detail the previous year and talk optimistically about the future. Jack Smit, President and CEO, tells them, "This is the New World. No borders. Unlimited access. Where emerging opportunities wait around every corner. Where the pitfalls, that few people discuss, are just as significant as the opportunities.

"It is thrilling. It is frightening," adds Smit. "It is the world that our children will inherit earlier than

Open Question Period at AGM, January 2000

any of us can imagine. We are in a world that is changing at warp speed."

January 22, 2000 is the dawn of a new century. Though the delegates are sitting in a hall that's only a few city blocks from where others sat one night to decide on the creation of St. Willibrord, they are almost 50 years removed from them. The delegates of today may be here for similar reasons, but the credit union at the beginning of the 21st century is clearly different in scope and style from what it was in the middle of the 20th. Probably no one who sat in the hall on Colborne Street, in 1950, ever dreamed that what was being created that night would turn into the multi-million dollar, high-tech organization of today. But throughout a long history, St. Willibrord has been forward-thinking, leading edge at times, and in recent years certainly confident of its place in the financial landscape of Ontario and Canada. On the eve of its 50th Anniversary, St. Willibrord is enjoying good times.

As Smit tells the delegates, "It is this new, wonderful, largely unpredictable world in which we have to find our place. Better yet, we have to build our place and establish our comfort zone. We have to create new ideas and new ways to prosper. Fundamentally, we have to lead.

"Leadership is a tradition at St. Willibrord, fostered by the owners who have always been a part of our credit union. People like

Twenty-fourth Annual General Meeting 1974

you. St. Willibrord was created by leaders. People who found themselves in another kind of new world, yet a new world just the same."

But what of the future? What direction does St. Willibrord take as it moves into its second 50 years and, along with the rest of the world, crosses the threshold to the 21st century? How will it change? What is its vision and what will it do to meet the future goals and objectives of owners, staff, and other stakeholders?

If Jack Smit's dreams of the future come true, then St. Willibrord, in another 50 years, could seem as changed to year 2000 delegates as the present organization would be to those original founders. "We see ourselves as very much a regional player responding to our communities, and providing more products than we used to," he notes.

That's not too different from the course St. Willibrord has charted for much of its history. The credit union is located in an area with almost two million people and, as Smit observes, "we are not even scratching the surface" of that marketplace. Although the credit union did extend its boundaries into Kitchener-Waterloo in 1998, Smit doesn't see it moving beyond its core area in the heart of Southwestern Ontario. However, he wants to reach a 15 per cent market share in the next 10 years, about *five* times the size the credit union is now. In other words, 150,000 owners. "That's ambitious," he admits, "but then, we've always been an ambitious credit union.

And I think we can." The key will be how well St. Willibrord does in first growing to 50,000 owners. The next few years will be crucial because Smit believes it's more difficult to grow from 30,000 to 50,000 than it is from 50,000 to 100,000.

Why? The relatively small market share St. Willibrord has today means fewer people know about it, and the result is a fairly small presence in the larger community. One reason people continue to use banks is that they do have a higher profile across the country and give people a feeling of security about their money. Although St. Willibrord has several branches throughout Southwestern Ontario, its presence in London, with three branches, is limited. Certainly, staff have taken a more aggressive approach in recent years in soliciting new business, and even 10 years ago they wouldn't have played such an active role in following up leads and inquiries as they routinely do now. If the credit union doubles the number of branches in London in the future, and puts them in high profile locations, then potential customers might start seeing St. Willibrord in a different light. The north and western areas of the city are probably ripe for new branches.

That doesn't mean the credit union has plans in place to build them, though. New branches can be costly, and St. Willibrord's high-tech banking has meant that people don't have to come into branch offices to do their business as much as before. On the other hand, Smit feels that people will still want the personal touch and interaction with those handling their money. "I'm not convinced that the majority of people will be comfortable dealing in cyberspace, even 10 years from now." He likens banking in the future to book shopping in the late 90s. You can order books electronically through a service such as chapters.ca, where you don't do anything more than click on items on your computer screen. But you also have the option of chatting with a well-read salesperson in a local bookshop and making a purchase that way. There is room in the marketplace for both methods. "Technology is a great enabler, but you never know how it will spin out. At a basic level, people still want to deal with people, particularly when it comes to their money. They want to have some comfort, trust, and a real relationship."

Smit envisions possibly smaller branch offices or storefronts in malls, which could handle people's needs without necessitating large capital costs and staffing. In 1999, St. Willibrord thought long and hard about where it wanted to locate its newest branch in the Kitchener-Waterloo area, ensuring that it be close to where members work and live and also show the cities that the credit union is there and doing business. “Visibility and accessibility are important,” Smit adds. That visibility will also apply to senior administrators who will be more involved in all communities where St. Willibrord has branches, but most notably London. More public appearances and sponsorship of community events all “contribute to the success of our community. And I think, 10 years from now, we will be doing more of that.” Board member Chris Nanni agrees, noting that St. Willibrord’s community presence is stronger in the smaller towns outside London than in the city itself. “We’re hoping to see more community involvement because it also lends itself to more owners coming through the door.”

Harry Joosten, Vice President of Owner Relations and Corporate Secretary, agrees that the 150,000 owner goal is possible. As the credit union expands, growth will become easier because more people will be directly involved in it or know someone who is. One challenge will be coping with possible increases in branches, branch councils, and even delegates, to ensure that people still feel connected and in control. New committees may have to be set up and councils might consist of like-minded owners who can work together to bring ideas to the administration instead of just those who happen to come from the same branch.

Word of mouth, which has always been crucial to St. Willibrord’s growth, will also continue to play a vital role. Current owners who talk about how well they are served by St. Willibrord remain, as Smit notes, “our best ambassadors”. But that may not be enough to fuel greater growth. If the credit union does expand that much, it’s likely, however, that some mergers with other credit unions in the area will take place. Joosten feels these organizations should be aware that St. Willibrord welcomes such mergers as a way of reaching its goal of being the number one source for financial service in Southwestern Ontario. “Every credit union should feel welcome. We think we have a good model, and anybody who wants to, is welcome to be part of it. The unique, fun part is that when they join, they themselves become part of the process of shaping where we go from here on.”

The administration and Board of Directors are on the same page about future growth. Board members Tony Strybosch and Chris Nanni look eagerly toward the future and St. Willibrord’s continuing success. With assets of half a billion dollars in 2000, the two were confident that could double in 10 years. Nanni wasn’t as sure about reaching 150,000 owners, but he does believe St. Willibrord provides such good quality service that existing owners will continue

Board of Directors 2000. (Left front) Tony Sleegers (Back row, l-r) Chris Nanni, Nick Groot, Pete Goertz, Ken Meinzinger, Marycatharine Kusch, Joanne Pollock, Tony Strybosch, Jim Poel

to do more of their financial transactions there. Strybosch, who's been on the Board since the late 80s, has seen phenomenal growth take place in those years and expects the same in the 21st century. "I think our future is very bright. The growth will be very dynamic."

Credit unions in the late 90s were also benefiting from people's disappointment in Canadian banks. High service charges, proposed mergers, and the closing of branches, were all things that worked in credit unions' favour. In fact, had the bank mergers gone ahead in 1998, Smit believes it would have benefited St. Willibrord and other credit unions. "The focus of the banks would have certainly gone more global than what it is now, which is good for us. And they probably would have closed more branches." But Joosten says that disenchantment is not something on which credit unions can continue to rely to spur growth. Although he's confident about St. Willibrord's growth beyond 100,000 members, what makes it stand out from banks is the personal service and control it can offer to people who are part of it. "The challenge, then, is when you reach that size, how do you stay close to each owner?"

That word "owner" is a crucial one, something which will be a more familiar part of the St. Willibrord lexicon in this century. In fact, the word "owner" was already showing up in St. Willibrord's marketing literature in the late 90s. The word "member" is still in the Credit Union Act, so St. Willibrord has to use it in some contexts, but in its thinking and marketing, "owner" is the word of choice. The credit union's Web site address, with the initials "mycu", short for "my credit union", is designed specifically to create feelings of trust, ownership, and comfort. "If you want to deal in person, plus on the phone, plus over the web, and you want it to always look and feel the same, if you want it all, then you'll deal with St. Willibrord," Joosten says. This concept of people owning the credit union helps St. Willibrord distinguish itself from other financial institutions. It also provides an advantage, adds Nanni. If you don't like the way a bank is doing business, you have little recourse to change how it operates, but as an owner of the credit union, you do have some power to make changes. "I think that's the edge that we still have," says Nanni. St. Willibrord also benefits from its delegate structure, which allows owners who are farther away from the administrative offices to feel connected and loyal. "If we don't retain that, I don't think we can go forward as dynamically as we are doing now," Strybosch adds. "But we work very hard to do exactly that."

Board Chair Tony Strybosch congratulates CUDA Graduates at AGM 2000. (l-r): Micki Angyal, Maureen Dunning, Ellen Smulders, and Peter Lenders

Other credit unions are picking up on the "owner" concept, too, and by the late 90s, it had certainly become an essential part of St. Willibrord's marketing strategy to attract new people. "Because you're an owner, it implies respect, empathy, proper deference to your wishes," Joosten explains. The idea also reinforces St. Willibrord's desire to strengthen relationships with its owners, but "the most important relationship is not the one you have with the credit union but the one you have with your money. If you feel better about your money, and your future, because of your relationship with us, then we're doing our job," he says. "That's key. It's your money and your future. We are your coach, your adviser, and your financial tool supplier. We cannot presume to be any more than that."

St. Willibrord will increasingly take on the role of what Joosten calls "integrator" for its owners. Being an integrator won't just be about cramming external and internal products together for its owners to choose from, but making sure they work together smoothly and cleanly. "As an integrator, we combine, organize and choreograph all the elements necessary to be our owners' source of quality financial services," says Joosten. "Source is a key word here. The credit union is the owners' source for products, for the channels through which they buy and use those products, for the information, advice and tools they need to set their goals, build their plans, implement them, and then monitor the results. Being an integrator allows you to extend almost everything: your product line, your market reach, your range of possible access and delivery channels beyond the current individual capacities of your single, individual credit union organization." This means owners will rely more and more on St. Willibrord in the coming years to provide them with the information and advice they need to have personal control over their money in a globalized world. It boils down to St. Willibrord making its owners feel comfortable about how their money is handled. "It feels like you're wearing your favourite sweater... not like a cold, hard bank," adds Joosten. "That's how we want people to feel." And as more people feel that way, and spread the word about this different kind of relationship, St. Willibrord hopes that will lead to more owners within the organization.

Of course, any change St. Willibrord experiences will be made in the context of the larger financial world and society in general. For example, the credit union watched with interest, in March 1999, when British Columbia members of the Surrey Metro Savings Credit Union overwhelmingly turned down a $131 million offer by Canada

Trust to buy its shares. Had that deal gone through, the members of the B.C.-based credit union would have joined forces with the larger, more national trust company. Then, without their having a single thing to say about it, they would have been swallowed by the TD Bank after its merger with Canada Trust. The offer had been endorsed by the Surrey Metro Board and management, but in many respects, the rejection by Surrey members was a wake-up call not just to Surrey's leaders but to other credit unions as well: Pay attention to what your owners want and don't simply follow the money! It sent a powerful message to "be very careful before you sell us out to a national company," says Smit. "[Owners were saying] we're dealing with you because you are local, you are part of the community, you're responsive to our needs. [They like to be able to say] I can go to the annual meeting, I can call Jack Smit on the phone and talk to him, and I can't do that with a national situation."

Joosten says the Surrey decision showed that owners are still in charge, and administrations at other credit unions must "not take the concept [of ownership] for granted. I don't think we have. I know we haven't." That's why St. Willibrord introduced a more "town-hall" format at its annual branch meetings in 1998 and 1999, encouraging as much feedback as possible. "That was part of our 'Picture Tomorrow' project in 1999. We wanted everyone, not just the Board and management but every branch councillor, and delegate, every staff member and even every owner to have a say, a chance to influence and shape St. Willibrord's strategic plans for the

Owners vote at AGM, January 2000

future." Using questionnaires, focus group and team discussions, and town-hall debates at the branch annual meetings, participants looked at the issues to be faced and the decisions to be made by the individuals, families, enterprises, and communities of tomorrow in Southwestern Ontario. These issues and decisions will be an important part of St. Willibrord's tomorrows as well. At the 60th Annual General Meeting of the Credit Union Central of Ontario in March 2000, St. Willibrord was recognized for this innovative program by receiving CUCO's first NOVA Award for Corporate Governance.

It is this inclusive, consensus approach that will carry St. Willibrord into the 21st century. "That's part of the reason for our success," says Smit. "We have a clear focus on our vision and mission, and it's shared extensively."

The desire to provide good service and stay close to owners is also what drives St. Willibrord's approach to the country-wide drive to develop a national service entity for credit unions. It was a big item on its agenda in 1999. Several credit union officials throughout Canada argued that a much more focused and national organization was needed to ensure that their financial institutions stay competitive with big banks and that more tightly-linked credit unions would allow owners better access to their accounts regardless of where they were in Canada. Such a restructuring could see the current structure of provincial and federal "centrals" replaced with a new national entity designed to improve delivery of service. Senior administration and Board members at St. Willibrord thought a great deal about what its position would be regarding such a national organization. On one hand, joining a strong national credit union body could give these financial institutions more clout and possibly save money on administrative duties. On the other hand, it could lead to a loss of identity and even control over how business is done locally. St. Willibrord was hoping for the best of both worlds. "What we want to happen is we want to remain a regional credit union and hope that we have a lot of other large, regional, similar-thinking credit unions across the country that will share resources in a national entity," explains Smit. "So the national group will be there to service the needs of the credit unions.

"Such an organization might be able to handle back-office tasks that credit unions don't need to take care of individually. For example, it doesn't make sense for St. Willibrord to have its own staff overseeing the investment of liquid assets. Of the $50 billion in total assets among credit unions in Canada, about $5 billion is liquid. A few people, working on behalf of a national group of credit unions, could handle investing that in the wide variety of specialized financial instruments that generate the best return while guaranteeing the principal and keeping it liquid. If there are 50 to 100 credit unions, why do you need 50 to 100 investment managers?" St. Willibrord, however, would take care of more crucial areas such as staff training and keeping owners satisfied. "So I want to keep the strategic things locally, and the non-strategic things, if there are benefits in economies of scale to do it together, on a national basis."

Without that regional control, St. Willibrord and other credit unions would become just like banks, Smit believes. Adds Joosten, "If it's a national service organization serving credit unions, which operate in their own communities and regions, that's fine. If we ended up being just a funnel for the [national entity] then I think we would have lost the whole concept of local community control."

As it turned out, the idea of a single, national, credit union service entity fizzled out in late 1999 and early 2000. Outside Ontario and Nova Scotia, there was not enough support among provincial centrals or the credit unions to go for a "big bang" approach to build such an organization. Instead, the credit union system has collectively identified six areas where it wants to see accelerated development: e-commerce, wealth management, services for small and medium enterprises, national branding or awareness, and consolidation and/or better efficiencies in the

THE CUDA PROGRAM

The Credit Union Director Achievement program encourages the development of skills necessary to function as an effective credit union director. It is designed by provincial credit union centrals, in conjunction with the Canadian Cooperative Association and the Credit Union Institute of Canada.

The goals of the program include strengthening the credit union system by offering opportunities to enhance the skills, knowledge, and abilities of credit union directors.

Those who are successful in the CUDA program have completed nine modules as well as three electives. Training related to CUDA may be accessed through seminars or correspondence, and some modules are also available in a computer-based format. Module topics for study include: Planning and Policy Making, Board Development and Performance Evaluation, Management Recruitment, Risk Management, and Leadership.

Roots and Branches *authors Mark Kearney and Otte Rosenkrantz prepare to gather comments at AGM 2000*

areas of liquidity and payments mechanisms.

St. Willibrord supports concerted actions in all these areas except branding, where it will be hard to develop a national consensus until the issue is much better defined and understood.

Regardless of how St. Willibrord is connected to any national organization, one thing is certain; it will continue to diversify services and products so that owners will have a wide range of choices. In earlier years, the credit union learned a lesson about relying too much on one sector of the economy or society for its growth. While its roots in agriculture remain strong, St. Willibrord expects to continue to broaden its base into the small business sector, mortgages, and mutual funds. By not relying on any particular segment of the economy, the credit union protects itself from a serious setback when one element of the economy experiences a downturn. It may also expand services into family trusts, estate planning, and brokerage.

If one thing is clear as St. Willibrord enters the second 50 years, it's that change is inevitable, and the credit union will continue to manage and adapt as it always has. The days of running the business out of someone's home, when a handshake was all that was needed to seal a deal, were fun, good-spirited, and exciting. But they were the good old days, and will remain a part of the history. In an increasingly complex world, St. Willibrord officials want to rely on the values from those days, but at the same time embrace the coming changes, and make them all work for them.

It is fitting, in a history of this credit union, where the Strybosch name has been so prominent, that a last word go to a Strybosch, in this case, Tony. Like many long-time members, Strybosch remembers the early days fondly, but knows that the days ahead will also be exciting, interesting, and rewarding for St. Willibrord owners.

"Some people say, 'St. Willibrord isn't what it used to be.'" Strybosch pauses a moment, for effect. "But we wouldn't want it to be what it used to be. It has to be with the times. However, it still has the very same intent, looking after our owners."

COMMENTS FROM OWNERS AT THE YEAR 2000 AGM

"Our family moved to Canada in 1954. There were nine kids altogether. In 1957, my Dad wanted to buy a house, and he needed to borrow $5,000, which he was able to get from St. Willibrord ."

Mary Sleegers

"I joined St. Willibrord in 1963 because of the hospital plan and the trips they organized to Holland. I started getting full banking services in 1981. I really like the personal service you get there. I don't care so much for electronic banking. What makes St. Willibrord special is the fact you can still go there and deal with a human being."

Chris Monden

"I joined in 1991 because of what I guess you could call my 'anti-bank' feelings. I like the sense of community we have here at St. Willibrord. I like the convenience of electronic banking, and I like the fact that there is not a constant turnover of the people I deal with. There seems to be a real sense of stability here."

Peter Cameron

"I've been part of the Credit Union since I was 10, since my father (John Féron) was president, and I can remember how in those days, the annual meetings were held at the Ukrainian Hall on Adelaide Street in London. Those meetings were really more of a social affair than a business meeting. There was a dinner and a dance, and it was a great opportunity to get together and socialize with family and friends. Now, of course, it is a large credit union and a successful business, and it has to have more formal meetings. But I hope we don't lose sight of where we came from."

Michael Feron

"I decided to join St. Willibrord about ten years ago after some friends recommended it to me. I have been very impressed by the people-oriented focus of the organization. I was the first member signed by [Account Manager] Andrew Brown at the London East branch, and we have become good friends since then. I can't imagine that happening at regular banks – the staff turnover is just too great."

Ray Chowen

"I have been a member of the Kingswood (Electrohome) credit union for 25 years. I was pleased when Kingswood joined with St. Willibrord because of St. Willibrord's reputation for stability. My credit union has been with me through good times and some not so good times, and they have not let me down. The credit union is great for small business."

Dave MacDonald

"I joined in 1955. I remember giving my deposits to John Strybosch in his house. I still have my very first deposit slip."

John Verkley

"The credit union was there when the early Dutch immigrants first came to this part of Canada, and it has been there ever since. I started John's Fruit and Vegetables here in London, and St. Willibrord was very helpful."

John Reyers

Epilogue: Still Growing

Janet Anderson's and Kees Govers' business is definitely growing. Not only in the sense that business is good and getting better and larger, but it is growing in the sense that the couple grows perennials, and lots of them.

"We carry 1,800 varieties of perennials," says Govers, "and ship them from Lansing, Michigan, to Cape Breton, Nova Scotia." With 14 full-time staff and six part-time people, and business growing by upwards of 25 per cent a year, Anderson and Govers own JEA Perennials, a highly successful business which, 13 years ago, was little more than a dream and a single, 16 by 100 foot polypropylene greenhouse.

"We started the business from absolute scratch in 1987," says Anderson. At the time, Kees was employed by Downham Nurseries in Strathroy, and Janet was working for Adrian Govers, Kees' father. Kees and his parents had come to Canada from the Netherlands in 1979, and Adrian Govers, who had been in the greenhouse business in the Netherlands, continued the tradition in Canada, growing annuals. "Adrian had no real interest in perennials, so I grew some on the side with the idea of selling them wholesale."

Janet and Kees met while they were at The University of Guelph completing Bachelor of Science (Agriculture) degrees and were married in 1986. In 1989, the young couple leased some property a few kilometres from their present location in order to expand their business. During four years in that location, they erected four additional greenhouses to keep up with the demand for their product. By the time they bought, and then moved to, their present location, they had seven greenhouses, which they moved with them. "We would never do that again," says Janet with a bit of a rueful laugh. "We did it hoping to save a little money, not realizing at the time that it would not be worth the effort. We would probably have been better off just getting new ones, but hindsight is always 20/20."

Since 1993, JEA Perennials has been located on 23 acres of land in Cairngorm, 4 km southwest of Strathroy, and business has been blooming. With 85,000 square feet under plastic, and more planned, JEA Perennials now supplies some of the most discriminating retailers in Ontario and beyond. "We have always been wholesalers," notes Kees. "Initially, we supplied about four garden centres around London, and then slowly expanded the business. About four or five years ago, we landed our first Toronto-area customers."

All of these garden centres were up-scale, medium-sized centres catering to a fairly demanding clientele, people who knew exactly what they wanted for their gardens. "These are not what we would call price-sensitive customers," says Kees. "We diversified into the types of products these clients wanted, as opposed to selling mass-produced product." Janet notes that "there are, for instance, some hostas which retail at $90-$100 a pot, and there are people who won't blink at that." She adds that this is actually one of the strengths of their product line because they don't have to compete head-on with other growers who produce more commonly purchased plants such as impatiens.

The types of products the couple produces are used in perennial beds and borders, hardy plants for the most part, but they also produce clematis, ferns, grasses, a few tender perennials, and shrubs, about 1,800 varieties in all, including 80 varieties of herbs. Thirty to forty per cent of their product line is produced from seed, either by them or by specialty seeders. Cuttings produce another forty per cent, about half of which are grown by JEA Perennials, and half by specialty cutting producers. And finally, twenty per cent is produced

Kees and Janet

by tissue culture laboratories. There are a number of such labs in the U.S., and a few in Canada, that supply a certain spectrum of product not readily produced from either cuttings or seed. Tissue culture is a viable way of multiplying these plants.

Spring is traditionally the busy season but, as Kees says, "The business is really year round, even though sales only occur from March to November, with the peak occurring during the eight-to-ten week window in the spring when we sell 85% of all the product. The rest of the year is spent gearing up to meet the anticipated demand."

Without question, the business continues to expand. Janet and Kees distribute their plants from Lansing, Michigan, to Ottawa, using their own trucks. They have also shipped orders both to Alberta and Cape Breton Island. But too much growth too soon is not always a good thing, and the couple had not expected their business to be this big this early in the game. "The business has to stay manageable," says Kees. "At some point, we will probably say that this is as large as we want to get." They have not yet quite reached a point when the growth has to stop, but they're getting close. As they say, there seems to be a threshold point in the volume of sales where an organization can become too big for the clients it already has. Both Janet and Kees feel they have grown with the market. As the popularity of gardening continues to increase, the business will also grow. JEA Perennials has experienced a jump of at least 25% a year in sales every year since they started. But of course, none of this would have happened without the right financial help.

St. Willibrord holds the mortgages on the JEA properties, and supplies the line of credit. "St. Willibrord is the only financial institution we do business with," says Kees. "We never got involved with any other." The couple started with St. Willibrord because Kees' father opened his accounts with the credit union after coming to Canada. When Janet and Kees went looking for money, they automatically went to St. Willibrord. "The first year I borrowed $2,000," says Janet. "And when we wanted to expand the business, we went to St. Willibrord. They were willing to take on a new, growing operation."

Part of the credit union's willingness to take on the account also had to do with the couple's ability to keep books and write clear business plans. They have made money every year they have been in business. "It wasn't much that first year," chuckles Kees, "when there were only 500 flats of plants, but in relative terms, as a percentage, we have always made a good profit."

One of the things they like about St. Willibrord is the stability of the institution. "You go to any of the big banks, and either the credit manager or bank manager changes every two or three years, and you have to teach the business to that individual all over again. In our case, with the credit union, we have had three account managers, and all three are still involved with the account to a certain extent. The branch manager has been there for more than 20 years. Nursery-greenhouse operations are very specialized, and require a good basic knowledge. We don't want to have to teach our business to new people all the time."

As for the use of Internet banking, they are not doing that much yet. "There is a certain satisfaction that comes with being able to go to the credit union at the end of May in person, with the account books, to show them how well we've been doing." Their day-to-day banking is also still done in person since, as Kees observes, "We like the human contact, and when there are decisions to be made, we still need to meet with people face-to-face."

The company grows significantly each year even though Janet and Kees would be quite content with a ten to twenty per cent rate. "Too much growth too fast is hard to cope with. If we try to do too much, we and the staff might burn out, and we might not be able to meet orders. The other factor is that we have 23 acres, and could build 15 acres of greenhouses. At $10-$15 a square foot, how much money could we afford to put into a business that has a 10-week sales period? There are about two acres under poly now and we could go to three. Beyond that, we would need a lot more staff, and it might not be good for growth. But any growth we might contemplate would certainly involve St. Willibrord."

The couple is eagerly anticipating the launch of their Web site in August or September 2000. The site will not be for commercial purposes," notes Janet, "because our market is wholesale. But it would be an information site for our customers, and for anyone interested in finding out more about what we do." Janet adds that the site will almost certainly be of special interest to customers wondering what kinds of plant material the couple has available.

As St. Willibrord Community Credit Union looks to the future, it does so remembering the importance of its rural roots. Janet Anderson and Kees Govers with JEA Perennials symbolize the many owners who have always been central to the credit union's success. Young, entrepreneurial, cautious but confident, comfortable with new technology but not given to jumping on technological bandwagons, future owners like this couple will no doubt help ensure the continued success of St. Willibrord.

APPENDIX 1

Chronology

November 14, 1950	– Memorandum of Association signed
January 25, 1951	– received Charter (Certificate of Incorporation)
July 26, 1951	– registration of first office at 1229 Dundas St., London
September 16, 1951	– opened branch at Wyoming (Sarnia)
November 13, 1951	– opened branch at Woodstock
November 22, 1951	– opened branch at Strathroy-Watford
April 1, 1952	– office moved to 100 Central Ave., London
March 15, 1952	– opened branch at Chatham
March 15, 1953	– opened branch at Stratford
October 1, 1953	– new office at 150 Kent St., London
March 17, 1955	– opened branch at Wallaceburg, which amalgamated with Chatham
May 23, 1961	– opened branch at Sarnia
November 7, 1962	– opened branch at Seaforth
April 1963	– board decides to have all correspondence in English (previously Dutch and English)
November 1963	– radio advertising approved on a trial basis on the Woodstock local radio
March 1964	– reached $1,000,000 in assets
September 1964	– sale of WIBO TravelService
November 1, 1964	– amalgamated Wyoming (Sarnia) and Strathroy-Watford branches into Arkona
March 1965	– joined Alliance of Dutch Canadian Credit Unions
June 26, 1966	– official opening of new office at 151 Albert Street
June 1969	– Fiscal Year End moved to September 30th

June 1970	– policy set outlining Rules and Regulations for Divisions
February 1971	– distinction made between current account and personal chequing account
September 30, 1971	– amalgamated Woodstock branch with London, and Seaforth with Stratford
April 1972	– purchase of computer, printer, and programming designed specifically for St. Willibrord
May 1972	– Rev. Father J. van Wezel honoured with the Royal Order by Queen Juliana of the Netherlands
April 1973	– information booklet entitled: "How service happens at St. Willibrord Credit Union"
1973/1974	– building projects for Arkona, Stratford, Chatham, and Strathroy branches
January 1974	– participate in television advertising plan for London and area credit unions
May 1974	– word "Division" changed to Branch and "Cashier" to Branch Manager
1975	– $10 million in assets
July 19, 1975	– opened new office for Arkona branch
September 1, 1976	– discontinue Grand Bend office
October 1, 1976	– first offered Plan 24 (daily interest savings account)
January 10, 1977	– opening of Watford branch office
May 1978	– Golden Club for seniors begun
1979	– $50 million in assets
May 3, 1980	– grand opening of new Blenheim office (merger of Chatham branch & Blenheim CU)
November 22, 1980	– opening of Dundas St., London, branch (office moved from Wharncliffe Rd., London)
December 1980	– Conversion to CUData software system completed, making all 8 branches online
March 1982	– new branch structure with delegate representation
October 1982	– introduction of The Personal 1® (chequing account)

August 1984	– St. Willibrord sponsors Ontario Co-Operative Young Leaders Program for the first time
March 1985	– introduction of MasterCard® II Payment Card
January 1986	– introduction of NestEgg savings account
September 1986	– St. Willibrord joins Interac® Network
June 1987	– St. Willibrord connected to Plus® System Network
June 1989	– participation in the Children's Miracle Network Telethon began
July 1989	– first issue of staff newsletter, called WillPower
March 9, 1990	– London South branch opens for business
June 1990	– first appearance of LTC bus painted in CU colours to commemorate 40th anniversary
October 1990	– introduction of Fat Cat® and Headstart® youth accounts
1990	– introduction of "Relationship Banking"
April 23, 1993	– grand opening of branch and administration office at 167 Central Ave
May 1993	– no fee MasterCard® Credit Card offered
April 1994	– new service package offered, called Extended Service Connexion™
May 1, 1995	– offering of Series 95 Class B Investment Shares – sold out in minutes
1995	– launch of Five Star Service Program - recognizing superior member service by the branches
November 1995	– launch of TeleService® (automated banking by phone)
January 1996	– first profit sharing distribution
May 28, 1996	– St. Willibrord's Vision: "We will be Southwestern Ontario's preferred source for quality financial service."
April 1997	– members receive a Service Quality Guarantee as part of their Service Agreement
June 1997	– opening of the Call Centre and addition of TeleService® Representatives
July 1998	– opening of Kitchener-Waterloo branch
August 1998	– launch of www.mycu.com

October 1998	– launch of Investment Services in partnership with MemberCare® Financial Services
January 1999	– conversion to new banking software system called Ovation™
March 31, 1999	– introduction of online, Internet banking
September 1999 to January 2000	– "Bright Ideas" Challenge '99: celebrating inventive thinking
June 30, 2000	– Recorded balance sheet assets exceed $500 million

APPENDIX 2

Year by Year Numbers

Year	Membership	Assets $	Net Income $	Loans $
1951	231	62,183	2,547	55,430
1952	585	185,526	2,590	173,860
1953	823	229,511	3,168	228,952
1954	1,069	251,837	5,958	233,068
1955	1,298	360,530	10,928	334,484
1956	1,608	527,205	14,307	490,614
1957	1,613	616,931	13,854	596,239
1958	1,850	714,154	16,079	666,478
1959	2,060	734,622	13,325	713,063
1960	2,393	751,182	16,964	661,659
1961	2,729	962,719	21,427	776,228
1962	3,087	923,802	28,369	842,775
1963	3,399	960,955	30,738	903,790
1964	3,766	1,091,983	34,432	936,881
1965	4,169	1,379,751	35,174	1,181,318
1966	4,642	1,790,058	31,053	1,575,227
1967	5,097	1,960,000	34,234	1,711,958
1968	5,586	2,410,598	21,221	2,064,002
1969	5,998	2,117,623	19,081	1,928,638
1970*	4,860	2,375,524	35,742	2,006,557
1971	5,027	2,827,897	80,165	2,467,513
1972	5,167	3,393,298	96,744	3,389,139
1973	5,565	6,017,738	119,542	5,024,045
1974	5,442	8,219,804	192,400	6,811,952
1975	5,907	13,172,169	263,438	11,032,818
1976	6,400	17,673,160	241,859	15,182,952
1977	7,298	25,263,373	272,915	21,020,907
1978	11,708	36,325,370	261,354	31,519,558

1979	14,071	50,248,902	8,767	43,837,511
1980	14,190	51,228,367	(706,591)	43,691,558
1981	14,261	54,688,242	(667,185)	44,879,596
1982	14,603	61,876,671	214,786	50,500,596
1983	15,628	77,513,919	189,684	66,182,938
1984	15,979	90,445,243	345,448	75,829,867
1985	16,605	103,970,690	367,415	88,485,082
1986*	15,917	109,642,663	325,415	91,234,435
1987	17,415	126,485,435	205,487	97,840,174
1988	18,562	142,037,389	451,391	116,010,014
1989	19,110	159,211,000	885,000	133,371,000
1990	19,852	186,288,000	660,000	159,694,000
1991	21,233	211,313,000	632,000	181,277,000
1992	21,451	240,450,000	848,000	203,350,000
1993	21,646	262,667,000	1,032,000	224,702,000
1994	23,624	298,029,000	1,400,000	252,308,000
1995	24,028	322,918,000	1,833,000	273,835,000
1996	24,714	348,512,000	2,304,000	302,060,000
1997	25,435	379,013,000	1,334,000	335,230,000
1998	28,748	431,484,000	1,451,000	375,461,000
1999	30,607	459,087,000	1,276,000	394,261,000

***Notes**

1970 – Fiscal Year was 9 months long due to change of Fiscal Year End to Sept. 30

1986 – Membership Shares implemented; method of counting members changed

APPENDIX 3

Founding Members:

John Verhallen	M. Minten
S. Perguin	Gerard vanden Boomen
W. J. Bontje	Martin Vlasman
G. Felix	L. Mulders
J. A. Scholten	L. C. B. Liebregts
Th. Beernink	F. van Bussel
J. J. Bontje	N. Stuifbergen
Chris De Vreeze	Henry Van Dinther
Martin vanden Heuvel	J. B. Bos
Jac. van Geel	J. P. Langeveld
(Rev. Jan van Wezel)	A. van Hees

President/Chair of the Board:

Siebert Graat	1951-1959
William Intven	1959-1970
John Féron	1970-1980
Henry Olsthoorn	1980-1983
John Timmermans	1983-1986
Nick Van Osch	1986-1998
Tony Strybosch	1998-present

Treasurer/General Manager/President & CEO:

Theodore Smeenk	1951-1952
Frederica Vanbrock (née Beretta)	1952
August Cammaert	1952-1957
Nicolaas Van Wijk	1957-1963
August Cammaert	1963-1966
Martin Verbeek	1966-1968
Walter Mutsaers	1968-1969 (acting)
John Strybosch	1969-1988
Jack Smit	1988-present

APPENDIX 4

Board of Directors

Name	Position Held	Dates Served
Siebert Graat	President 1951-1959	July 24, 1951 – Jan 29, 1959
Gaston Legon	VP 1951-1952	July 24, 1951 – August 10, 1952
Ted Smeenk	Secr-Treas 1951-1952	July 24, 1951 – October 26, 1952
Steve Perguin		July 24, 1951 – August 7, 1953
John Vande Werf		July 24, 1951 – October 26, 1952
Bill Fox	VP 1952-1953	August 10, 1952 – February 15, 1953
August Cammaert	Treasurer 1952-1953 Secr-Treas 1953-1956	October 26, 1952 – December 15, 1956
John Strybosch	Secr 1952-1953 VP 1953-1956 VP 1960-1963	October 26, 1952 – February 12, 1956 May 15, 1960 – March 24, 1963 November 7, 1968 – February 4, 1969
Theo Beernink		February 15, 1953 – February 17, 1957
Theo Versteegh	VP 1956-1959	August 7, 1953 – February 25, 1962
Adrian Groot	VP 1959-1960	February 12, 1956 – May 15, 1960
William Intven	Secr 1956-1959 President 1959-1970 Secr 1970-1984	December 15, 1956 – January 16, 1988
Jack Boere		February 17, 1957 – March 24, 1963
John Féron	Secr 1959-1970 President 1970-1980 VP 1989-1991	January 29, 1959 – January 15, 1994
Harry Brouwers	VP 1963-1966	February 25, 1962 – March 6, 1966
Alphons Kerkhaert	VP 1967-1970	March 24, 1963 – November 27, 1970
Peter Van Engelen	VP 1966	March 24, 1963 – November 27, 1970

Name	Position Held	Dates Served
Henry Olsthoorn	VP 1971-1972 VP 1974-1975 VP 1978-1979 President 1980-1983	March 6, 1966 – January 18, 1997
Adrian Bruijns	VP1972-1974	November 7, 1968 – January 22, 1981
Harry Vossen	VP 1970-1971	June 20, 1969 – November 26, 1971
Nick Verbeek		November 27, 1970 – November 24, 1972
Peter Van Bree		November 27, 1970 – November 25, 1976
Harry Hak		November 26, 1971 – November 23, 1974
Tony Sleegers		November 24, 1972 – present
John Van Kessel	VP 1975-1978	November 23, 1974 – January 18, 1978
John Timmermans	VP 1980-1983 President 1983-1986	November 25, 1976 – January 20, 1987
Paul Kiteley		October 1, 1977 – January 17, 1980
Nick Van Osch	President 1986-1996 Chair 1996-1998	October 1, 1977 – January 16, 1999
Bert Segeren		January 18, 1978 – January 22, 1981
Lou Rivard		January 17, 1980 – January 18, 1986
Henry Van Kessel		January 22, 1981 – January 21, 1982
Don Van Goozen	VP 1984-1989	January 22, 1981 –January 18, 1992
Jack Smugler		January 21, 1982 – January 12, 1985
Ray Hanson		January 12, 1985 – January 18, 1986
Chris Nanni	VP 1991-1996 Vice-Chair 1996-present	January 18, 1986 – present
Herman Van Bakel		January 18, 1986 –January 16, 1993
Tony Strybosch	Chair 1998-present	January 16, 1988 – present
Adrian Van Engelen		January 16, 1988 – January 15, 1994
Arnold VanderHelm		January 18, 1992 – January 17, 1998
Anne Callon		January 16, 1993 – January 14, 1995
Pete Goertz		January 15, 1994 - present
John Van Noort		January 15, 1994 – January 22, 2000
Jim Poel		January 14, 1995 – present
Nick Groot	2nd Vice Chair 1998-present	January 18, 1997 – present
Joanne Pollock		January 17, 1998 – present
Marycatharine Kusch		January 16, 1999 – present
Ken Meinzinger		January 22, 2000 - present

APPENDIX 5

Credit Committee

1951-1996

John Aarts
Theo Beernink
Ted Donkers
G. Guichelaar
John Hendrikx
Firmin Matthys
John Roks
Gerald Sanders
William Schreurs
Tony Sleegers
Cornelius Smeekens
Nick Stokman
Chris Van Bree
Antoon Hees
William Van Niekerk
Martin Vanden Boomen
John Vlasman
Harry Willems

APPENDIX 6

SUPERVISORY COMMITTEE

1951-1996

Peter Aarts
Theo Beernink
Jack Bontje
Alastair Brent
Harry Brouwers
Maria Bruijns
Marinus De Rond
Harry Giesen
Adrian Groot
William Intven
Alphons Kerckhaert
Joe Liebregts
Tony Marsman
Tony Sleegers
William Strik
Martin Van Geleuken
Frank Van Loon
John Vande Laar
Nys Vanden Dool
Tom Vermue
Chris Walraven

APPENDIX 7

Branch Councillors

At the Annual General Meeting in January 1982, St. Willibrord Community Credit Union formally adopted bylaws which instituted the control structure based on Branch Councils and Delegates with which the credit union still operates today. The first elections for Branch Council and Delegates took place in November 1982 at the Branch Annual Meetings. At that time, the Branch Councils formally replaced the Branch Advisory Committees in each branch. The names listed below are for those persons who have served as a Branch Councillor in each branch from 1982 to the present, arranged in alphabetical order. (See also Appendices 8 and 9)

Blenheim Branch 1982-present	Stratford Branch 1982-present	Strathroy Branch 1982-present
Linda Clendenning	Gary Bokkers	Andy Bruijns
John Cowan	Peter Bokkers	John De Groot
Michael Feron	Ron Boyce	John Dortmans Jr.
Ken Gardiner	Antoon De Groot	Judy Farr
Jerry Kempe	John Gras	Peter Goertz
Liz Meidlinger	Marie Huitema	Lyle Hendrikx
Arnold Nooyen	Aleida Stinnissen	Lorraine McLeod
Dan Nooyen	Herman Van Bakel	Earl Morwood
Jack Van Aert	William Van Westerop	Tony Slegers
Betty Van Haren	Ernest Vander Schot	Nick Stokman
Gerald Van Lith	Arnold Vander Wiel	Geraldine Van Hoof
Dave VanRaay	Madeleine Visser	Diane Vander Velden
	Henry Wydeven	Ray Wiendels

London Branch 1982-1989	Arkona-Watford Branch 1982-1989	Sarnia Branch 1982-present
Dan Baljet	Jerry Beernink	Betty Alderman
Alastair Brent	Ray Hanson	Jeanny Astolfi
Ted Donkers	John Hendrikx	Leo Bartelen
Pat Eveland	Tony Hogervorst	Brad Brownlee
Dan MacDonald	Charles Page	Mary Clemence
Henry Motton	John Peters	Peter Crombeem
John Roks	August Roelands	Ludger De Bont
Philip Squire	Gerald Sanders	Ted Deelstra
Audrey Timmerman	Bruce Shelley	Trudy Ladanchuk
John Van Noort	Leo Straatman	Mark Lumley
Arthur Van Waterschoot	Peter Van Engelen	Matthew Mitro
Bert Verbeem		Kathy Perdeaux
		Theresa Ridland
		Halbe Taekema
		Don Van Goozen
		John Van Werde
		Arnold Vander Helm
		Louis Vandersteen
		Art Wallace
		John Wolfenden

Arkona Branch 1989-present	Watford Branch 1989-present	Kitchener-Waterloo Branch 1998-present
Jerry Beernink	Ralph Bakker	Ron Heimpl
Gerald Cates	Leo Bongers	Phyllis Lichti
Arnold Kester	Terry Bryson	Ken Meinzinger
Allan Nethercott	Ross Daly	Philip Pfeifer
John Peters	Kathy Ikert	Laraine Whaling
Gus Roelands	Bert Sanders	
Tom Sangster	Leo Straatman	
Teresa Van Bree	Cathy Van Dreumel	
Peter Van Engelen	Jeff Van Eyk	
John Verkley	Don Van Gorkum	

Albert St./Central Ave./ London Downtown 1989-present	Dundas St./ London East 1989-present	Southdale/ London South 1990-present
James Beretta	Bart De Vries	Cheryl Barber
Rob Bondy	Ted Donkers	Ron Bokkers
Alastair Brent	Nick Groot	Maureen Dunning
Anne Callon	Rick Joyal	Ruth Edwards
Kathy Coulson	Dorothy Kassies	Michael Feron
Don Cumming	Henry Motton	Brad Geddes
Bev Dawson	Jim Poel	Stephanie Haggerty
Pat Eveland	Shirley Scarrow	Walter Hanisch
Mike Feron	Ellen Smulders	Al Hughes
Peter Noble	John Snyders	Joe Kester
Rob Pelletier	John Van Noort	Bette McGoldrick
Bill Strybosch	Bert Verbeem	Kevin Morrison
Cindy Webster		
William Willcock		

APPENDIX 8

Branch Delegates and Alternates

As noted in the preamble to Appendix 7, the first Branch Delegates and Alternates were elected in November 1982. From 1982 to 1996, the designated number of runners-up in the Branch Delegates elections (two or three, depending on the size of the branch) were elected as Alternate Delegates. Alternates voted on behalf of their branch in place of Delegates who could not attend the annual General Meeting. At the Annual General Meeting in January 1997, the Delegates and Alternates voted to eliminate the Alternate position. The names listed below are for those persons who have served as a Branch Delegate and/or Alternate from 1982 to the present, arranged in alphabetical order. (See also Appendices 7 and 9)

Blenheim Branch
1982-present

John Blonde
Henk Boekhorst
Jack Boogaart
Dick Buitenhuis
Peter Cameron
Linda Clendenning
Pete De Bruyn
Tony DeJager
Ann Dorssers
Mike Feron
Paul Horak
Ted Jarecsni
George Kernohan
Marvin Laidlaw
John Lugtigheid
Guy McCreery
Elizabeth McDonald
Elizabeth Meidlinger
Chris Monden
Chris Nanni
Erick Nooyen
Rick Pilkey
Bert Segeren
Bill Sluys
Claire Taylor
Leo Timmermans
Steve Uher
Jack Van Aert
Bert Van Lith
Gerald Van Lith
Debbie Verhart
Leo Verhart
Reinout Von Martels
Elaine Warriner
Tony Wiltenburg
Ben Zegers

London Branch
1982-1989

Arnold Arts
Dan Baljet
Ron Berman
Harry Beukeboom
Joyce Bree
Al Brent
Harry Brouwers
George Brown
Anne Callon
Ernest Cowan
Don Cumming
Bart De Vries
John de Vries
Bob Deane
Marian DeCaluwe
Gerry Delange
Marinus DeRond
Miel Devries
Gabriel DeWaal
George Dykhuis
Ed Eade
Patrick Eveland

Paul Ewald
Barbara Farr
Barry Fay
Mike Feron
Fred Gale
Ivor Griffiths
Peter Haasen
Shirley Ham
Karl Hobyan
Rita Hodkinson
Harry Hoevenaars
David Hooper
Iva Humble
Martin Joldersma
George King
Don Koebel
Mary Kolkman
Marie Langeveld
Gerry Larocque
Marg Larocque
Dan MacDonald
Eleanor Mercer

Henry Motton
Johannes Pol
Frank Pyka
Jan Richardson
Frank Rodgers
John Roks
Hans Rosch
Shirley Scarrow
Willem Smulders
John Snyders
Henry Stam
Art Stelpstra
Muriel Stilson
Phil Thatcher
Audrey Timmerman
Barb Turner
John Van Noort
Andre Van Stigt
Art Van Waterschoot
Bert Verbeem
Ed Vroon
John Zadorsky

Arkona-Watford Branch
1982-1989

Ralph Bakker
Nancy De Groot
Gerhard Eilers
Rod Glen
Henk Goertz
Calvin Hartley
Henry Maas
Allan Nethercott

John Peters
Tony Rombouts
Wayne Runnalls
Tom Sangster
Tony Strybosch
Christine Van Bree
Elsie Van Bree
Adrian Van Engelen

Don Van Gorkum
Peter Van Loon
John Vander Burgt
Frank Vander Kant
Chris Vander Vloet
Phil Venema
John Verheyen
Leo Wouters

Sarnia Branch
1982-present

Cornelius Akerboom
Betty Alderman
Jeanny Astolfi
Bill Ballard
Leo Bartelen
Tina Bax
Arie Bezemer
Maurice Braet
Brad Brownlee
Peter Crombeem
Art De Groot
Gerald De Jong
Ted Deelstra
Jan Elderhorst
Jacob Feenstra
Kathy Furlotte
Chris Greydanus
Bert Hoogendam
Jim Lovell
Tony Magermans
Matthew Mitro
Carl Modderman
Frank Murphy
Jake Pama
Kathy Perdeaux
Sharon Raaymaker
Theresa Ridland
David Rogers
Morris Schenk
Andy Sleeuwenhoek
Halbe Taekema
Norma Unsworth
John Vanden Broek
George Vandenberg
Arnold Vander Helm
Anthony Vander Steen Jr.
Louis Vandersteen
Paul Vandersteen
Mike Virsotek
Andrew Walsh
Connie Willems

Stratford Branch
1982-present

Kim Ahrens
Stuart Baker
Larry Batte
Ann Boersen
Peter Bokkers
Frances Cook
Bill Cozyn
Jack De Groot
Paul de Groot
Tony De Groot
Frank Eckhardt
John Gras
John Houben Jr.
Marie Huitema
Peter Huitema
Harry Hulman
Vince Hulsof
Tony Hunter
Wilma Jilesen
Herman Koert
George Masur
Bill Mayberry
Patrick Murray
Peter Neal
Karen Nyenhuis
Ben Nyland
Mathew Peters
Ivan Roobroeck
Gerry Snyders
Aleida Stinnissen
Jay Thistle
Herman Van Bakel
Henry Van Heesch
Jim Van Herk
Marian Van Klooster
Josie Van Moorsel
Peter Van Nynatten
Bill Van Westerop
Leo Vande Wetering
Ernest Vander Schot
Madelaine Visser
Henry Wydeven

Strathroy Branch
1982-present

Micki Angyal
Wilma Aris
Marilyn Bach
Dan Baker
Elizabeth Breimer
Andy Bruijns
Chris Crump
John De Groot
John Dortmans Jr.
Anne Giesen
Harry Giesen
Peter Goertz
Malcolm Gray
Don Green
John Groom
Dominic Haasen
Lyle Hendrikx
Margaret Hoefnagels
Mike Joosten
David Kettlewell
John King
Betty Kirkness
Marycatharine Kusch
Tony Kustermans
Jennifer Langford
Victoria Langford
Peter Lenders
Edith MacGregor
Linn Marron-Marshall
Ross McKenzie
Lorraine McLeod
Peter Minten
Earl Morwood
Cathy Seward
Harry Slegers
Tony Slegers
Ed Thuss
Ted Thuss
John Timmermans
Martin Timmermans
Anthony Van Deven
Geraldine Van Hoof
Eric Vandenheuvel
Gerry Vander Hoek
Diane Vander Velden
Mary VanderVloet
Anthony Vandeven
Mary Verberne

Albert St./Central Ave./London Downtown
1989-present

Cindy Bakker
James Beretta
Harry Beukeboom
Louise Beukeboom
Michael Beukeboom
Jack Blocker
Jeff Boere
Rob Bondy
Charlotte Bouckley
Jeanette Bree
Yvonne Brown
Lois Cote
Kathy Coulson
Don Cumming
Bev Dawson
Peter De Groot
Martin De Rond
Gabriel De Waal
Marian DeCaluwe
Beth Dinardo
Susan Eagle
Denise Hallam
John Henry
Bob Hoevenaars
Harry Hoevenaars
Michael Lamb
Richard Lyke
Jon Mackenzie
Connie Marshall
Kelly Matthews
Rick McCombie
Peter Noble
Bob Peel
Rob Pelletier
Frank Pyka
Jan Richardson
Neil Ripley
Jim Romanow
Michael Ryan
Heinrich Spies
Henry Stam
Owen Thornton
Michael Tremblay
Harry Van Bavel
John Van Bommel Sr.
Richard Vande Wetering
Annette Vanden Boomen
Scott Wellman
William Willcock
William Zweers

Dundas St./London East
1989-present

Shaffiek Abdool
Arnold Arts
Dan Baljet
Peter Beerda
David Arthur Broad
George Brown
Ray Chowen
Jim Cole
Bart De Vries
Marty Donkers
Lois Eagleston
Ray Eaton
Barry Fay
Nick Groot
Tom Harris
Florence Heeman
Doug Hill
Joy Jackson
Rick Joyal
Dorothy Kassies
Maureen Khan
Don Koebel
Marie Langeveld
Dan MacDonald
Jerry Martens
Karen Meyer
Henry Motton
Katrin Nagelschmitz
Pam Nielsen
Ronald Partridge
Jim Penders
Jim Poel
Joe Pol
Cristal-Lynn Reed
Hans Rosch
Frank Schreurs
Bill Smulders
Frank Snyders
Muriel Stilson
Audrey Timmerman
Peter Timmerman
Mavis Van Boxmeer
Bert Verbeem
Ernie Verbeem

Southdale/London South
1990-present

Ron Berman
Ron Bokkers
Joyce Bree
Michelle Brock
Lorne Campbell
Maureen Dunning
Earl Flynn
Terry Gallivan
Henry Guetter
Stephanie Haggarty
Dianne Hamilton
Lori Joseph
Ian Ketelaars
Gerry Kuhfus
Lynne Matthews
Art McCann
Tom Mistretta
Mary Owsiak
Marvin Recker
Frank Serratore
Gary Siroen
Muriel Stilson
Frank Verkley

Arkona Branch
1989-present

Jim Bouma
Cheryl Campbell
Gerald Cates
Pete De Vet
Gerhard Eilers
Henk Goertz
Arnold Kester
David Marsh
John Muller
Allan Nethercott
Bob Peters
Gary Peters
Karen Quinn
Tony Rombouts
Barb Smeekens
John Smits
Martin Thuss
Tina Thuss
Teresa Van Bree
Frank Van Der Kant
Chris Van Der Vloet
Henny Van Kessel
Anne Vanos
John Verkley
Harry Willemse

Watford Branch
1989-present

Mary Lou Acton
Terry Bryson
Violet Caley
Annie Clark
Ross Daly
Marilyn Faris
Jack Geerts
Rod Glen
Chris Gordon
Carolynne Griffith
Wendy Hollingsworth
Kathy Ikert
Jane Joris
Kevin Marriott
Carl Migchels
Randy Molzan
Darren Munro
Gordon Richardson
Wayne Runnalls
Bert Sanders
Frank Van Den Ouweland
Cathy Van Dreumel
Brenda Van Engelen
Jeff Van Eyk
Pete Van Loon
Phil Venema
Harold Willcocks
Lawrence Zavitz

Kitchener-Waterloo Branch
1998-present

Bill Johnson
Rev. Al Kehn
Lisa Lackenbauer
Dave MacDonald
Ray Popplewell
Ed Weidinger

APPENDIX 9

Advisory Committees

As noted in the preamble to Appendix 7, Branch Councils formally replaced Branch Advisory Committees in November 1982. The names listed below are for those persons who served as a member of a Branch Advisory Committee for the applicable branch, arranged in alphabetical order. Not all branch committees were in operation for the entire period from 1951 to 1982. As can be seen from the variety of branch names, it is clear that many branches (or "divisions" as they were earlier called) were constituted for much shorter periods of time during the first thirty years as they were established, amalgamated with other branches, grew and split into separate branches or offshoots, or closed outright.

Sarnia
-1982

Leo Bartelen	Martin Raaymakers	John Van Werde
Jack Boere	Fred Rusticus	John Vanden Broek
Maurice Braet	Halbe Taekema	Antoon Vander Steen
John Brouwer	Harry Van Boxmeer	Martin Verbeek
Ludger De Bont	Don Van Goozen	Frank Verbeke
Piet De Meyer	A. Van Leugenhagen	John Verheyen
H. Donkers	August Van Loy	Henry Vossen
Martin Magermans	William Van Ommen	Frank Wigchert
Jake Pama	Arthur Van Waterschoot	

Strathroy
-1964

Annie Aarts
Andy Bruijns
Adrian Groot
John Hendrikx
Joe Michielsen
Harry Naus
John B. Peters
Cornelius Smeekens
Nick Stokman
John Strybosch
Jerry Swart
Peter Van Engelen
Chris Van Loon

Arkona
1965-1974

Adrian Groot
August Huyben
Joe Michielsen
Harry Naus
John B. Peters
Cornelius Smeekens
John Strybosch
Peter Van Engelen
Ted Van Eyk
Chris Van Loon
August Van Loy
John Vanden Broek
Theo Verwegen
John Willemse

London
-1982

Truce Brouwers
Adrian Bruijns
Arnold Damen
Ted Donkers
Alphons Kerkhaert
John Langeveld
Dan MacDonald
Harry Meulendyks
Brian Parsons
John Roks
Robert Sexsmith
Tony Sleegers
Steve Steinbacher
Audrey Timmerman
Gerard Tromp
Frank Van Doorne
Arthur Van Waterschoot
Len Vanden Berg
Nys Vanden Dool
Nick Verbeek
Huib Vergeer
Jacob Vermue
Harry Willems
Mathys Witlox

Woodstock
-1971

Antoon Does
P. Does
Robert Geelen
Jack Oosterveer
Andy Op de Weegh
Jim Penders
William Schreurs
Gert Slykerman
Theodorus Tuns
John Van Gerwen
Rein Van Lierop
Adrian Vander Pas
Anton Vander Vleuten
John Verhoeven
John Vernooy
D. Vreeker
Theodorus Vreekler
John Wortel

Stratford
1953-1982

Ysbrand Boersen
José Cozyn
Jules De Brabandere
Antoon de Groot
Jack De Groot
Paul de Kroon
Pieter French
Pieter Klomp
Mary Leyser
Peter Leyser
Gerard Nyenhuis
Leo Savelberg
Leo Tovenatti
Pieter Van Herk
William Van Westerop
Gerard Vanden Broek
Gerald Vanden Hengel
Arnold Vander Wiel
Chris Walraven

Seaforth
1963-1971

John Groot
Harry Hak
John Lansink
Jack Renne
Martin C. Van Bakel
John Willems

Chatham
1952-1979

Harry Blommers
Bernard De Brouwer
L. De Brouwer
Gerard De Bruyn
Peter De Bruyn
Jerry Kempe
Jules Modderman
Arnold Nooyen
Gerard Olsthoorn
Cor Philipi
John Ryken
Bert Segeren Jr.
Bert Segeren Sr.
Betty Van Haren
John Van Haren
Bernard Van Lith
Walter Van Pinxteren
John Van Raay
Rene VandeWynckel
Chris Westelaken
Harry Wijsman

Arkona-Strathroy
1976

Harry Naus
August Roelands
Cornelius Smeekens
Peter Van Engelen
Chris Van Loon

Arkona-Strathroy-Watford
1977

John Hendrikx	August Roelands	Chris Van Loon
Harry Naus	Peter Van Engelen	

Arkona-Watford
1978-1982

John Hendrikx	Charles Page	Peter Van Engelen
Lorne Hodge	August Roelands	Chris Van Loon

Blenheim
1980-1982

John Cowan	Jerry Kempe	Claire Taylor
Ken Gardiner	Arnold Nooyen	Betty Van Haren

Wyoming
1962-1964

Jack Boere	Martin Gerrits	Ted Van Eyk
Bert Donkers	William Raaymakers	August Van Loy
H. Donkers	Harry Van Boxmeer	John Vanden Broek

APPENDIX 10

Name Changes

Dutch Catholic Immigrants (London) Credit Union (January 1951)
    1952: discussion of name change to St. Willibrord
St. Willibrord (London) Credit Union Ltd. (1953)
St. Willibrord Credit Union Limited (1975)
St. Willibrord Community Credit Union Limited (1983)

Mergers – all through Purchase and Sale Agreements

Co-op Services (London) Credit Union — October 1, 1977
    (became Wharncliffe Road branch, subsequently moved to London East on Dundas Street in 1980)
Blenheim Community Credit Union — January 2, 1980
    (combined with Chatham branch but location kept Blenheim)
London Container Employees Credit Union – July 31, 1982
    (added to London Downtown branch)
London and St. Thomas Real Estate Board Credit Union – August 1, 1983
    (added to London Downtown branch)
St. Joseph's Parish (Sarnia) Credit Union – October 15, 1983
    (added to Sarnia branch)
Inwood Community Credit Union — July 31, 1984
    (added to Watford branch)
No-Sag Employees (London) Credit Union — August 15, 1984
    (added to London East branch)
Spartan Employees' (London) Credit Union — April 15, 1985
    (added to London East branch)

Brewers Warehousing Employees (London) Credit Union
– October 31, 1986
(added to London Downtown branch)
St. Joseph's Parish (London) Credit Union — August 31, 1987
(added to London Downtown branch)
Steelworkers Foundry Employees (London) Credit Union — March 31, 1988
(added to London East branch)
Dominion Chain Employees (Stratford) Credit Union — April 30, 1988
(added to Stratford branch)
London Comet Credit Union — October 1, 1993
(added to London Downtown branch)
Northern Employees' (London) Credit Union — November 30, 1993 [Northern Telecom]
(added to London South branch)
Campus (London) Credit Union — October 1, 1994 [U.W.O.]
(added to London Downtown branch)
Kingswood Community Credit Union – June 30, 1998
(became the Kitchener-Waterloo branch)
BFG Employees (Kitchener) Credit Union – May 31, 1999
(added to the Kitchener-Waterloo branch)

Index

A

B

D

E

F

G

M

N

T

U

V

W

Y

Z